SALES
CAREERS

The **ULTIMATE** Guide
to Getting a High-Paying
SALES JOB

EDWARD R. ("TED") NEWILL   *and*

LOUISE M. KURSMARK

jist
Works

Sales Careers: The Ultimate Guide to Getting a High-Paying Sales Job

© 2003 by Edward R. Newill and Louise M. Kursmark

Published by JIST Works, an imprint of JIST Publishing, Inc.
8902 Otis Avenue
Indianapolis, IN 46216-1033
Phone: 1-800-648-JIST   Fax: 1-800-JIST-FAX   E-mail: info@jist.com

Visit our Web site at www.jist.com for information on JIST, free job search tips, book chapters, and how to order our many products!

Quantity discounts are available for JIST books. Please call our Sales Department at 1-800-648-5478 for a free catalog and more information.

Acquisitions and Development Editor: Lori Cates Hand
Cover and Interior Designer: designLab, Seattle
Page Layout: Trudy Coler
Proofreader: Deb Kincaid
Indexer: Tina Trettin

Printed in Canada
07 06 05 04 03   9 8 7 6 5 4 3 2 1

Library of Congress Cataloging-in-Publication data is on file with the Library of Congress.

We have been careful to provide accurate information in this book, but it is possible that errors and omissions have been introduced. Please consider this in making any career plans or other important decisions. Trust your own judgment above all else and in all things.

Trademarks: All brand names and product names used in this book are trade names, service marks, trademarks, or registered trademarks of their respective owners.

ISBN 1-56370-959-7

ABOUT THIS BOOK

If you've picked up this book, you're probably interested in joining the nearly 16 million people in the U.S. who hold jobs in some area of sales. For the right person, a sales career is a great choice. Most sales jobs offer tremendous flexibility and the chance to directly influence your earnings. That's right—the harder and smarter you work, the more money you'll make, based on the commission structure of most sales jobs.

This book will help you determine whether a sales career is right for you. In chapter 1, we provide a thorough introduction into sales—its definition, terminology, and nuances for different industries. Then we clear up some common misunderstandings by exploring what *isn't* sales. This chapter is an important foundation to the rest of the book, and we recommend that you read it in its entirety. Then you might want to skip around through the other chapters, focusing first on the areas in which you're most interested.

Do you want to know more about what a sales career is really like? Read chapter 2, "What's Great and What's Tough About Sales," then move on to chapter 3, "A Week in the Life of a Sales Professional," where you'll follow in the footsteps of three successful salespeople. "Why Women Rule in Sales," chapter 6, includes vignettes of nine women in industries that range from automobiles to real estate to apparel.

Of course, you'll be interested in chapter 4, "What Does a Sales Job Pay?" But before you decide to make a career move, be sure that this is the right field for you. Chapter 5, "The Art and Science of Sales: Understanding and Assessing Your Fit for the Field," thoroughly discusses traits and characteristics necessary for success and then provides a checklist so that you can perform your own self-assessment. And finally, in chapters 7 and 8, we'll guide you as you break into sales and advance your career.

Each chapter ends with a "Wrap-up and To Do" list to help you make immediate, practical use of what you've learned. The appendix includes valuable resources you can use as you continue to explore this exciting career field.

CONTENTS

Introduction		**ix**
Chapter 1:	**Defining Sales**	**1**
	What Is Selling?	2
	What Isn't Sales	5
	Are You Already Selling?	6
	A Wide Variety of Selling Environments	6
	The Sales Cycle	9
	Types of Sales Positions	10
Chapter 2:	**What's Great and What's Tough About a Sales Job**	**17**
	What Is Great About a Sales Job?	18
	What Is Tough About a Sales Job?	22
Chapter 3:	**A Week in the Life of a Sales Professional**	**29**
	A Week with Bud Zuberer, Senior Automation Consultant for a Leading Pharmacy Automation Company	29

A Week with Peirce Ward, New England
Financial Network   35

A Week with Kathy T.—from Teacher to
Sales Manager   40

Chapter 4: What Does a Sales Job Pay?   47

Sales Compensation Overview   48

Pay Ranges   56

How Does Compensation Affect Your Move
into Sales?   57

**Chapter 5: The Art and Science of Sales:
Understanding and Assessing Your
Fit for the Field   63**

The Art of Sales   64

The Science of Sales   69

Other Important Traits and Skills   78

Putting It All Together   80

Where Do You Learn the Art and the Science?   85

Career and Personality Assessments   87

Recognizing Your Balance   89

Self-Assessment Checklist   89

Chapter 6: Why Women Rule in Sales   91

Women's Traits for Sales Success   92

Successful Women in Sales: Nine Portraits   94

Chapter 7: Strategies for Breaking Into Sales 109

Where the Jobs Are: Strategy and Industry
Recommendations   110

The Dale Carnegie Course as a Proving Ground 115

Why Companies Hire 116

Selling Yourself in Your Resume and Cover Letter 118

Selling Yourself Through Networking 138

Selling Yourself in Interviews 139

Chapter 8: Sales Career Paths **153**

Initial Success 154

Careers in Direct Sales 155

Transitioning from Sales to Marketing 166

Transitioning from Sales to Sales Management 169

Transitioning from Sales or Marketing
Management to General Management 175

**Appendix: Resources for Your Sales Job
Search and Career** **181**

Career Assessments and Personality Type Profiles 181

Researching Employers and Industries 182

Top 10 Sales-Job Web Sites 184

Resources for Resume Writing and
Career Services 184

Resources for Sales Professionals 185

Index **187**

INTRODUCTION

Over the years, hundreds of people have asked us what a sales career is like and how to get into the field. Answering the same questions time after time gave us the idea for this book—in which we address those common questions and also tackle several important questions that people don't know to ask.

From personal experience and extensive contact with sales professionals at all levels, we can tell you that sales is a great career. Independence, financial reward, travel, recognition, camaraderie, fun... there are few careers like sales. It can be a most rewarding career personally and professionally, *for the right kind of person*. Yet we've found that sales is one of the most misunderstood of all careers. That's why we wrote this book—to help you understand just what a sales career is all about, whether you are "the right kind of person," and whether this career is right for you.

Ted's Story

In 1976 I was 23 and on the verge of completing grad school. If you had told me at that time that I was going to spend the bulk of my career in sales before ending up in the position of president of a company, I would have told you that you were absolutely nuts. I thought

(continues)

(continued)

I was interested only in general business management. My first job, a sales position, was going to be a step toward that goal. What I thought was going to be a step turned into a very satisfying career. The same opportunity might be out there for you.

Louise's Story

That same year, 1976, fresh out of college and considering my options, a sales career would have been dead last on any career list I made. Instead, I pursued jobs in public relations and writing and, several years later, started my own business writing resumes and preparing various business documents. Through that experience, I discovered that some of my favorite people were salespeople, and now the "sales" part of my job (which is critical to the success of my business) is my absolute favorite. You might find yourself taking just such a roundabout path to a full-time career in sales.

What's in This Book?

In the following chapters, you will learn about the pros and cons of a career in sales. You will also learn about the personality traits and skill sets needed to succeed in sales. A very important part of the book gives consideration to sales career strategies. Some people don't understand how many different types of careers the word "sales" encompasses. You will learn about the multitude of careers available, the ones for which you are best suited, and how you can create and follow an upward career path.

There is a section on how to approach a company for a position. Here, you will learn important points about your cover letter, resume, and participation in the interview. Finally, you will get some guidelines for fitting into your new job and managing your efforts.

This book is particularly important for those considering a career change. Trying to get into sales mid-career can be a very frustrating experience. It is the old "chicken and the egg" problem. We don't know how many times we have heard the exasperated question, "How can I get any sales experience if no one will give me a chance?" There are solutions to this problem and strategies to follow. These are discussed at length with concrete examples of actions you can take to position yourself for a successful move into sales.

This is not a sales *rah-rah* book that is designed to talk you into a sales career by artificially boosting your ego or your confidence with a lot of psychobabble. Making a career mistake can be tragic for the individual and the company he or she is attempting to represent. For the individual, a failure in any career can create a poor self-image that is undeserved. Ted could try his hardest to be an architect but would probably fail. His inability to succeed would not be because he lacked important values such as a strong work ethic, integrity, and team play. He would fail because he doesn't have the right skill set, experience, and personality characteristics to succeed as an architect. Yet in this failure, he might let himself believe that he is a failure at everything in life. While this isn't true, it is human nature for people to be hard on themselves. You don't need a failure if you can avoid one. Ted doesn't need one either, so you won't see him interviewing for a position as an architect.

If you decide to try sales as a career, it is important that you find a sales role that is appropriate for your character traits and skills. Even within the sales profession it is possible to find a bad fit. An old college roommate's first sales job was a disaster. He just didn't fit. He could have given up. He didn't. He found a position with a medical company and did well in his second sales job. To help you find the right fit, we explore many different types of positions within the field of sales, devote some attention to personality assessment, and give you tools and information to help you match your profile to the right career options.

We have designed this book to answer many of your questions about breaking into sales and to provide practical steps to get you headed in the right direction. We have also made sure that it paints a realistic picture of sales as a job and a career. You don't have to read the chapters in order. After you read chapter 1, you can jump around to your heart's content. Enjoy the book and learn about a career that we have found very rewarding.

What Is the Future for Sales Careers?

What about the future? Will the Internet or some software technology eliminate sales jobs? Not a chance. Nothing replaces human contact. The computer and the Internet are, however, changing the way salespeople work. They are making selling more sophisticated. Also, technology companies and whole new industries have created thousands of new sales positions. Overall, the outlook for sales careers is bright. According to the *Occupational Outlook Handbook,* published by the U.S. Department of Labor, sales occupations are expected to grow by nearly 12 percent (1.9 million new jobs) by 2010.

Building a sales career is hard work, but the rewards are great. For some of you, a new career will start as you continue to turn the pages. Best of luck!

CHAPTER 1 Defining Sales

D efining Sales" is a cornerstone chapter to this book. Because it lends important perspective to the rest of the book, we recommend that you read this chapter first. After completing it, feel free to bounce around from chapter to chapter.

We'll start by defining sales or selling. Then we will talk about what *isn't* sales. This is important because many business activities that people tend to associate with selling are not what we consider sales from a career standpoint.

Also, just as there is a wide variety of engineers—chemical, mechanical, industrial, electrical, and so on—there is a variety of types of sales. This is important. As you can imagine, one individual might make a better chemical engineer than industrial engineer. This could be due to personality traits and particular skills—chemistry versus statistics, for example. In the same way, sales careers span many industries. And a sales career in one industry can be quite different than in another. We will explore this so that you can begin thinking about which industry or sales type is most appropriate for you. In later chapters we will provide more tools to help you determine the best steps to take to build a sales career.

What Is Selling?

Sales is the process of convincing another person or entity that you have a product and/or service that satisfies a need of theirs. The result is that they will give you something in exchange for your product and/or service.

This simple definition is really loaded with meaning. Let's break down the sentence more carefully.

"Sales Is the Process..."

Professional salespeople follow a process when interacting with a potential client. It doesn't matter whether the professional is a cosmetics specialist behind the counter at Nordstrom or a McKesson Automation sales representative selling pharmaceutical-management services to a hospital. There is a process they follow to understand the needs of the client. The client can be a 53-year-old female accountant who needs makeup or a hospital system that wants to better manage the distribution of prescriptions to the thousands of patients it cares for every year.

Salespeople start with some fact finding. At Nordstrom, the cosmetics specialist will probably ask the accountant about the clothes she likes to wear. Through some friendly discussion, she will try to determine the woman's style. What has she used in the past that she liked and disliked? What is her personality type—outgoing? laid back? What is her knowledge about skin care? What is her skin type—dry? medium? oily? And there will be many more questions. What will emerge is a picture of what this woman needs.

"...Satisfies a Need of Theirs..."

Now we are moving into another important part of the definition. What has happened so far? The cosmetics specialist has **asked questions** and **listened carefully** to the answers. She has also carefully watched her customer and observed her body language. Note that the specialist has not tried to sell anything. This is critical. At this point the cosmetics specialist is prepared to suggest a number of different products that will satisfy the needs she has uncovered.

"...Convincing Another Person or Entity..."

Finally, we are at the point of "convincing another person or entity...." The cosmetics specialist will explain to the woman how one or more products will satisfy her needs. She will also prompt her customer to make a purchasing decision. "Would you like the three-ounce bottle size or the six-ounce bottle?" "Would you like extra mascara for your purse?" "If you buy the makeup system I have suggested, you will qualify for a gift bag. Does this sound good to you?"

Sales Process and Methods

Of course, this sounds like a lengthy process. Sometimes it is, and sometimes it isn't. By demonstrating professionalism and asking thoughtful questions, the cosmetics specialist gains her customer's trust and interest in spending more time looking at cosmetics. Or the customer might have said she was in a hurry and needed to pick up an item and leave. A professional salesperson will still ask one or two simple questions while finding the item. "How is your supply of lipstick?" "Summer is here. Do you have a small tube of facial sun block to carry in your purse?" One might think that these are manipulative questions. Not at all. They are great questions. They are inquiring about the needs of the customer. The specialist will get more sales this way and satisfy the customer's need. Her customer might say, "Thanks, I do need some sun block. What do you recommend?" This last exchange might have taken less than three minutes.

For the McKessen Automation representative, the sales process might take three months to two years. This representative might have to talk to a dozen people involved in the decision-making process at the hospital—purchasing personnel, pharmacists, nurses, and doctors. Each of these groups of people has different needs. The doctor needs a product that helps effectively take care of the patient. The nurses need a product that is effective with the patient and also works well on the various patient floors. The pharmacist is concerned about different needs in different parts of the hospital. The purchasing manager needs a price and payment process that fit the hospital's budget as well as a good service program for the product.

Now think about selling a new computer system to a manufacturing company with 8,000 employees and six locations spread out across the world. That sales process is bound to be even lengthier and more complicated than selling to the hospital.

In all cases, the basic definition of sales holds true. Sales can be a very simple five-minute process between two people at a counter in a store. Or it can be a very lengthy and complicated process involving dozens of different people in several different locations. In complicated selling situations, a company might employ a group of people to do the job of selling. This would be a "sales team." The team selling the computer system might include a senior salesperson, a junior salesperson, a systems-integration specialist, a software engineer, and a hardware engineer.

The form of communication that we have assumed in the preceding examples is face-to-face interaction. In today's high-tech world, the definition of sales can be satisfied using mail, phone, or Internet as well as in-person communication. Selling over the phone is quite controversial—many people equate telephone sales with dinnertime harassment by telemarketers. But in fact, professional *telesales* or *telemarketing* people meet the criteria of a sales professional. A great example is the telesalespeople you will encounter if you call RoadRunner Sports or Dell Computer. In those calls, you will talk to very knowledgeable folks who will ask a lot of good questions so that they can offer you a product that fills your needs. On the other hand, if you call L.L. Bean, you will talk to a very friendly and highly trained *customer service representative*. The L.L. Bean representative is not engaged in telesales or telemarketing. He or she is merely processing your order. Consider the difference when you call Dell. You might have a particular computer in mind, and if so the representative will gladly take your order for it. But a good Dell sales representative will ask you some questions to determine how you are going to use this computer. After listening to your answers, the Dell representative might try to convince you that a different computer will better fit your needs. This is selling.

You have noticed that we have used the word "professional" to describe all of the salespeople mentioned in the preceding examples. Anyone who works hard to understand the success elements of their job and apply those elements diligently is a professional. Joe Montana was the consummate professional quarterback. He carefully studied the art and science of his game. Salespeople can be professionals, too. Those who are have very satisfying careers, both emotionally and financially.

What *Isn't* Sales

Now that you understand what sales is, let's talk about what isn't sales. The reason it is important to talk about what isn't selling is to kill the myth that sales is a second-rate occupation. Unfortunately, in real life, TV, and movies, the image of the slimy salesman is repeated over and over again. The true profile of a professional salesperson is the complete opposite of the image frequently played out in the media or that you experience from telephone harassment in the middle of your dinner.

Taking orders is not selling. If a clerk in a department store simply meets the customer at the cash register and rings up a purchase, the clerk has merely taken an order. Through its convenient location, advertising, and/or coupon programs, the department store has done all the selling. The customer arrived, selected a product that filled his need, and made the purchase. The selection process was done without the help of a knowledgeable employee of the store. The cashier might have a name tag with the title of "sales clerk" or "sales associate." But this really isn't selling.

Pressuring someone into a purchase decision is not selling, either. This is the typical image most people have of selling. It is the "used-car salesman" image. Or perhaps the door-to-door vinyl-siding salesperson image. Or the vacuum-cleaner saleswoman image. Remember, if handled correctly, each of these examples could be turned into the correct image of selling. Unfortunately, many people have been exposed to a number of high-pressure situations like these that are very uncomfortable. And they had a right to feel that way.

They were dealing with people more interested in how much money the customer could "pay per month" than in satisfying real needs.

Telephone harassment is not selling, nor is it true telemarketing. We call it "tele-spam." It is not much different from the spam you get on the computer. It is simply fishing for dollars. Tele-spammers will call as many people as they can until they get a lonely, trusting soul on the line and talk that person into buying a product or service they don't need. This is not selling. Be very careful to avoid a job like this if you are taking your first step into sales. As noted earlier, there are very good and very professional telesales and telemarketing career opportunities with reputable firms.

Are You Already Selling?

You might have realized as we defined sales that you are already selling. Most likely you are. When you convince a loved one, friend, or business colleague that your plan of action is the best, you are selling. You have listened to their position, and you have presented the benefits of your plan.

When this happens, do you frequently sway the decision in your favor? Do you enjoy persuading people to see things your way? If so, you might have some natural selling ability.

A Wide Variety of Selling Environments

In the next sections, we will begin to explore the wide variety of sales types. We will use certain products, industries, and companies as examples to help you understand what we mean. For those of you new to the idea of sales, the next few pages might seem confusing at first. In the end it will all come together. For those who are more experienced in sales and considering where you are in your career, this might be the place to begin to re-evaluate what sales roles you are best suited for.

While reading the next few pages, pay attention to how you feel as you read. Which sales situations feel comfortable? Which ones alienate you? If you are meant for a career in sales, you will more than likely be most successful in a particular group of industries and in a particular sales role. For example, one individual might be very successful selling valves and control systems to large chemical manufacturers. That same person could be a complete failure selling commercial insurance to those very same chemical manufacturers.

Selling Tangibles or Intangibles, or Both

A tangible product is something you can put your hands on. A truck, a surgical laser, a computer monitor, a tube of lipstick, a telephone... these are all tangibles. An intangible is harder to define and harder to "get your hands around." Insurance for the truck, an extended warranty for the surgical laser, a service maintenance agreement for all the computer monitors at a company, the usage plan for the telephone... these are intangibles.

A truck is something you can touch, sit in, and test drive. Because customers can see it, they can clearly imagine the truck's ability to handle a payload, travel in certain conditions, and comfortably seat the driver and passengers. They can also appreciate the available colors, styles, and options. The salesperson can actually demonstrate most of the features and benefits of the truck directly to the customer.

The insurance for the truck is a completely different matter. Now the insurance salesperson has the challenge of getting the customer to imagine a future and unforeseen accident or incident where insurance will be a benefit. This is intangible. A customer who has never been in a major accident has no concept of how a good insurance policy will protect her health, property, and financial well-being. How does one imagine the difference between a $250 deductible and a $1,000 deductible? How does one predict whether or not he will need $250,000 in property-damage coverage versus $500,000? It is very difficult. This is the challenge the insurance salesperson has when helping a customer make these decisions. This is what is called a *conceptual sale*. We will go into that more in the paragraphs ahead.

Now, more than ever, salespeople are asked to sell a tangible and an intangible together. This is the result of companies deciding that a product is much more than what is in the box. A very good example of this is the business of extended warranties. When you go to Sears to purchase a refrigerator, you are probably thinking about several things. The part of your buying process that deals with tangibles is going to be evaluating the proper size, color, and features of the refrigerator. Do you want side-by-side doors? Do you want an icemaker? The intangibles will be the reputation of the Kenmore product, the warranty that comes with the purchase, and the ease of getting the fridge serviced. Then the salesperson asks whether you would like an extended warranty. First, the salesperson was selling you the tangible product. Now he has shifted gears and must get you to imagine out into the future life of the product where some unexpected and costly service might be needed.

Mature Products Versus New-Concept Products

Another way to look at some product categories is whether or not they are mature products or new-concept products. A good example of a mature product is a bar of soap. Everyone needs to wash. Frequently, their first choice will be a bar of soap instead of liquid soaps. Bar soap has been around for over 100 years. Nearly everyone uses it. Products that have existed for a long time and have wide acceptance are considered mature products.

A new-concept product has not been available before or for very long. Typically, it is a new way of doing something. And it requires a new technology that we are not used to. Digital cameras are a good example of new-concept products. The idea behind a digital camera is to take a picture. It looks like a normal camera. But the way it is used is different, and the process of creating pictures is very different and not necessarily convenient. On the other hand, one can be very creative with digital cameras and the software that comes with them. Prices for new-concept products tend to be higher than for mature products. You could consider the film camera a relatively mature product. Like soap, almost everyone has a film camera. And they are much less expensive than a digital camera.

As you can imagine, new-concept products are more difficult to sell than mature products. Some people are better at and more excited about selling new-concept products. Others would prefer the mature products. This is important to consider as you make career choices in sales. Different personalities and skill sets are meant for these different product classifications.

Let's look at some more comparisons of mature and new-concept products within the same product category.

Mature	New Concept
Film camera	Digital camera
TV	Digital TV
Stereo system	MP3 player
Gas-powered car	Hybrid gas-electric car
Car insurance	Vacation insurance
Datebook	Digital organizer

Within both of these classifications you can find tangible and intangible products.

The Sales Cycle

When considering sales-career opportunities, it is important to understand the sales cycle of the companies and the products you are considering. The sales cycle is the time required to start and finish the selling process. Selling cycles can be as short as a few minutes or as long as several years. A Mary Kay or BeautiControl cosmetics specialist might have a sales cycle of three weeks if she is doing a home party. First, she convinces someone to host the party. Then, for the next couple weeks, she might assist the host with invitations and other advice. The party actually takes place, and she presents a number of products. Finally, several women take her advice and purchase various products that meet their needs.

Selling someone an insurance policy might take three months. Selling a manufacturer several new plastic-molding machines might take one year by the time needs are understood, specifications agreed upon, bids offered, a final bid accepted, and the machines delivered. An advertising agency might work for years to break into a new account.

Different sales cycles are meant for different selling personalities. Some people enjoy the ability to sell something every day. Others enjoy the thrill of the giant sale every few months.

Types of Sales Positions

There are many different types of sales positions that are defined by the kind of product to be sold, the environment in which it is best sold, and the expertise necessary to sell it.

Inside Sales

A high-quality piece of furniture is not something that a salesperson can put in a briefcase and carry into someone's home. Most people want to see the furniture. This naturally means going to a furniture store. The salespeople you would meet there have what is called an *inside sales* position. They are located in a store or office where the customer most often comes to them. Other inside sales positions would be auto sales, clothing sales, appliance sales, audio/video sales, and so on. These are salespeople you deal with every day when you do your shopping. There are also inside sales positions in a number of industrial businesses such as construction products and materials. Often, inside salespeople communicate with their customers by phone rather than in person. This is particularly true for business-to-business inside sales such as the construction products and materials companies just mentioned.

Retail Sales

The furniture store is also a good example of *retail sales*. These are sales made to the public. For the most part, they are at the end of the sales chain. Something sold retail is not meant to be resold.

Wholesale Sales

If we take the furniture-store example one step backward, we begin to enter the realm of *wholesale sales*. A furniture store usually represents several brands of furniture. When the manufacturer of each brand sells to the retail store, it is wholesaling its products.

Field Selling

Field selling requires going to meet your customer. Most of the time, the meeting takes place at the customer's place of business. For pharmaceuticals and medical products, this means going to the doctor's office, the hospital, and/or the surgical center. Real-estate agents meet their clients at the home that is for sale or drive the clients from one home to another. Someone selling industrial machine tools will be calling on the management and engineers at a manufacturing plant. A person selling Longaberger baskets will most likely be in a host's home presenting the baskets to a small group of friends invited by the host. Many field salespeople work out of their homes.

Technical Sales

Technical sales positions are found across all industries from retail audio/video to telecommunication products. The level of technical difficulty and the nature of the technical skills involved varies widely. A technical sales position doesn't always require an engineering, chemistry, or computer-science degree. However, it requires a technical aptitude so that the representative can intelligently discuss the product with both technical and non-technical people. For example, sales of surgical instruments is considered technical. The instrument-sales specialist has to be able to discuss instruments with doctors and nurses. She might have to observe surgery and advise the surgeon or nurses on the proper handling of the instruments. At the retail level, a sales associate at an audio/video store has to be able to understand the complicated features and benefits of dozens of products such as digital cameras, DVD players, and stereos. Furthermore, this person has to keep up with the rapid change in these products. To do this, he will rely heavily on another technical sales specialist, the *manufacturer's representative*. Every audio/video personal electronics store has representatives from various manufacturers such as Sony, Mitsubishi, Olympus, Kenwood, and Panasonic visiting regularly to sell the retail specialist on their products through persuasive education. The manufacturer's rep tries to be sure the retail rep knows everything about the products.

Relationship Sales

Some sales positions require a person with strong relationship skills. Typically, this involves repeat customers who are buying from the company on a daily, weekly, or monthly basis. The customer has a regular relationship with the supplier. And the supplier's image and relationship to that customer is embodied in the sales representative. Many times salespeople in this role become an integral part of the customer's business. They are not only responsible for selling products, but also for coordinating all other services and contacts with the manufacturer. Many customers like having only one person to deal with. This is called *relationship sales*.

Ted's first sales job was for a medical device company. The products were sold to doctors and hospitals. These devices were used regularly in surgery, so the doctors and hospitals expected to see Ted on a regular basis. This was a combination of high-tech and relationship selling. Also, and very important, Ted had absolutely no experience with these products prior to joining the company. His only knowledge came from some biology and anatomy courses in high school and college. The company provided all the training necessary to help Ted discuss these technical products intelligently with the medical professionals he called on.

Capital Equipment Sales

Products described as capital equipment require the expenditure of large sums of capital or money to acquire them. This kind of sale typically involves machinery and equipment used in manufacturing plants. It can also mean large, expensive office equipment. In the medical industry, it would include everything from surgical lasers to MRI machines. A replacement engine for a Boeing 757 is capital equipment. The cost of capital equipment can range from $5,000 to $10 million or more. Believe it or not, there are some manufacturing systems that cost millions of dollars. A capital equipment salesperson leads the sale of this equipment. In chapter 3 you will read about Bud Zuberer, who sells medical capital equipment. Finally, this kind of equipment is not sold to an end consumer. This is why car sales are not considered capital equipment sales.

Capital equipment can span the range of low-tech to high-tech, and mature products to new-concept products. It can be inside sales or field sales. Across the board, capital equipment has a longer sales cycle than consumer or disposable products. And the number of units sold tends to get lower as the price of the capital product gets higher. This is because higher-priced products require more time and effort to sell. Also, the unit demand in the marketplace for the larger and more expensive capital equipment is smaller. For example, in one year a machinery company might expect to sell only 24 manufacturing systems that cost an average of $8 million. They might employ six sales executives to do this. Each executive is responsible for selling four systems per year. On the other hand, a sales representative for a simple surgical-laser system costing $15,000 might be expected to sell 60 lasers per year or five per month.

One-Time Sales

One-time sales involve a product that will last a long time and require little future involvement with the customer on the part of the salesperson. Car sales are a good example. In most cases, once you buy the car, you rarely see the salesperson again. You might come back to the car dealer several times a year for service, but the salesperson won't be involved in your future service in any way. Another example would be some types of capital equipment (see the preceding section) such as packaging equipment for a manufacturing plant or an enterprise-wide computer system costing millions of dollars. This is especially true if the manufacturer has a small offering of products with exclusive features. A customer who buys from this manufacturer might not need to purchase another similar product for years.

B2B and B2C Sales

Finally, there are two terms that are commonly used in resumes and job descriptions to define the type of selling based on who your customer is. If you are selling to a business user, you are performing *business-to-business* (B2B) sales, whereas if you're selling to a consumer, you're engaged in *business-to-consumer* (B2C) sales. All of the types of selling we've discussed in this chapter fit into one of these two categories. And sometimes you might be required to perform both types of sales in the same job. For instance, Louise most often engages in B2C sales, promoting resume packages directly to the executives who will be using them. But sometimes she must put together a sales presentation for a company that is laying off employees and wants to provide outplacement services to its departing executives. In those cases, she is engaged in B2B sales, and the information, presentation style, package of services, and price can vary quite a bit from the B2C presentation.

Wrap-up and To Do

You have learned that sales can be simple and sophisticated. You are also starting to realize that you might be in selling situations in your everyday life. When you convince your family to see a particular movie, you are selling. Or when you make a presentation to your business colleagues to persuade them to accept a proposal, you are selling. When you talk your teenager into wearing a more appropriate outfit to a social event, you are selling.

You are also beginning to see that selling is a profession that spans all industries and includes many different types of sales positions. Of course, there is a lot of overlap in the types of positions described in this chapter. Each sales position has its own characteristics. It is important for you to understand them so that you will know where you will best fit.

A sales job at CompUSA is a technical, new-concept, retail, inside-sales position. A job selling computers in the business division of IBM is a technical, non-retail, relationship-oriented, field-sales position.

Selling cosmetics for Mary Kay or BeautiControl is a relationship, low-tech, mature-market, retail position.

Here are some ideas to help you zero in on the types of sales positions that are the best fit for you.

1. Start paying attention to all the products around you.

2. Try to figure out how they came through the chain of sales events and finally into your home or your place of business.

3. Ask friends who have sales jobs to describe their positions in the terms we have detailed in this chapter.

4. Every time you have one of these conversations, take note of your gut reaction. Is the job interesting to you? Does it sound exciting?

5. Are you already selling your ideas to loved ones, friends, and colleagues?

6. If so, do you enjoy the process of selling?

CHAPTER 2 What's Great and What's Tough About a Sales Job

Every career has its good and bad points. Often, a person looking into a new career does so with limited information. This information might be from a friend or based on personal observations that are not complete. The result is a "grass is greener on the other side of the fence" attitude. In this chapter, we are going to review the variables that make a sales job great and others that could make it tough.

Ted's Perspective

Much of this chapter has been developed over the years as I've talked to nurses who questioned me about getting into sales. Because my career is in medical devices, I spend a lot of time in surgeons' offices and operating rooms. Nurses frequently tell me of their interest in medical sales. Then they ask me for my advice. Many are confident they would be successful at sales for several reasons. First, they know the application of the medical device inside and out. They are also highly trained in anatomy, sciences, and patient care. Finally, they are very familiar with the customers: nurses, surgeons, and hospitals. When they see a well-dressed Ethicon (a division of Johnson & Johnson) sales representative drive up in a nice car, they think, "I could do that job better than she does. How much does she know about sutures, instruments, and surgery?"

(continues)

(continued)

As you will continue to learn, there is a lot more to sales than just "knowing" the products or industry. To succeed in sales, one must be able to convert that knowledge to action. A salesperson must also be able to live in the sales environment. Very few outsiders really know what this environment is like. It is my goal to give you that insight, because it has always been an important part of my answer to these nurses.

I should note that many nurses have moved successfully into sales careers. Several RNs have worked for me, but I have also talked a few out of making a big mistake.

What Is Great About a Sales Job?

There are lots of great things about sales. They include the following:

- Money
- Recognition
- Competition
- Independence
- Camaraderie
- Fun

The following subsections detail each of these positive aspects of a career in sales.

Money

Financial reward shouldn't be the only reason to pursue a sales career. But the fact is, salespeople are some of the highest-paid professionals in the workforce. When I was the VP Sales at Mentor H/S, at least one third of my salespeople made more money than I did! In some industries, the top sales reps of a company earn more than its president! In my industry, medical devices, it is normal to see annual sales incomes of $85,000 to $300,000. Now remember, a sales income is not a salary. It is a combination of salary and commission or straight commission (more on this in chapter 4).

Of course, not all sales positions are paid as well as my examples. However, salespeople make a better living overall than many other vocations and professions. Salespeople get paid for their efforts. This is one reason why people who have been introduced to sales and are successful at it rarely return to non-sales positions. Do well in sales and you can be very happy financially.

Recognition

Recognition is another great part of most sales positions. Depending on the company and industry, salespeople are recognized for their achievements yearly, quarterly, monthly, and sometimes weekly. Salespeople have personalities that enjoy attention and a feeling of accomplishment. There is nothing like seeing a memo that has been sent to most of your company's executives with YOUR name on it saying that YOU have exceeded your sales goals. There is nothing as sweet as being at a sales meeting and being asked to come up to the podium to receive an award for overachieving your goals for the year. Imagine it! You might be walking past 10, 30, or 200 of your sales colleagues on your way to the stage. The room is full of applause for YOU. People are shaking your hand, slapping you on the back, and giving you high-fives. When you take the stage, a camera might flash as a picture is taken of you receiving the award.

Recognition is a wonderful and very motivating experience. It is an important part of the process of working with salespeople. The most successful companies have very active recognition programs. If you find yourself in a company that does not recognize the efforts and successes of the sales team in an upbeat, motivating way, go find another sales job!

Competition

Competition is another big driver for successful salespeople. These professionals enjoy competing with others and also tend to compete with themselves. They also have to go head to head with other companies whose sales forces are offering competitive products or services. Typically, salespeople end up knowing the reps of the competing companies. In fact, it is good to know your competition well. At the same time, many salespeople enjoy competing with the other members of their own sales team. How does this happen? Typically, as a form of recognition, companies will rank their salespeople according to their sales achievements. Sometimes these rankings are published on a monthly basis. No one likes to be on the bottom of a ranking list. So the members of a sales team tend to vie with one another to be number one or in the top 25 percent. The most exciting competition is for the "Salesperson of the Year" award. Managed correctly, these can be very healthy, productive programs. They can also be the source of a lot of good-natured teasing among the salespeople.

Real pros compete with themselves as much as they compete against others. How do they do this? They set goals to strive for. The goal might be to make a certain amount of money or to sell 20 percent more of a particular product than in the previous month. They find an immense amount of satisfaction in achieving these self-imposed goals.

Independence

Many sales jobs require the salesperson to call on customers alone. Some salespeople work out of their homes. These opportunities are often called "outside" or "field" sales positions. Many salespeople like the autonomy of working away from their corporate headquarters. They don't have a supervisor watching their every move or poking a head in the office several times a day.

In many companies there is an unwritten rule: If a salesperson is hitting her numbers, don't ask how she spends her time. This rule can apply to inside salespeople as well as outside salespeople. If you are disciplined enough to take good care of your customers and achieve your goals, many companies will not hassle you over the details of how you spend your time. If you need to slip out to run an errand, attend a parent-teacher conference, see the doctor, or reward yourself with a 45-minute break at the driving range, this will be allowed as long as you keep up your end of the "rule."

Another aspect of independence is the opportunity to virtually run your own business. Think about it: your own business without the hassles of ownership. You make the sales to the customer accounts that you manage. You place many of the orders. You follow up to be sure your customers are happy. You direct the interaction of your company with customers in a particular area. You essentially have exclusive rights to sell national-brand products in a certain geography or to a particular list of customers. If you sell Kraft foods to grocery stores in Augusta, Georgia, you are running Kraft's business in this market.

Camaraderie

Have you ever belonged to a group of people that became very close knit? This group could have been a military unit, a sporting club, a family, or a high-school, college, or adult athletic team. Typically, a tight bond forms as the group works together to overcome emotional, psychological, or physical challenges. The resulting interpersonal chemistry creates deep feelings of intimacy, friendship, mutual trust, helpfulness, and respect. You become true comrades and experience camaraderie.

A well-managed sales organization creates an environment that inspires camaraderie among the sales team. It is the foundation on which very rewarding, lifelong friendships can be built. This camaraderie is another great thing about being in sales.

Fun

The best job is one that is enjoyable. Plainly said, sales can be a lot of fun. For every tough or negative customer, there are several who are a pleasure to deal with. Once you have paid your dues in your territory, some customers will treat you as a credible and respected consultant. They will ask you for your advice.

For example, Ted was at a Sears department store the other day. He wanted to deal with a specific appliance salesperson and was willing to wait 20 minutes while the salesperson finished with another customer. Ted could have easily dealt with another salesperson, but because he had worked with this man before, he trusted him. It must have made the Sears salesman feel great to know that people were willing to wait for him! Why was Ted willing to wait? Because from previous experience with this salesman, he knew that he was knowledgeable, pleasant, and professional. Later, the delivery and installation he organized went without a hitch. Chances are this salesman is having fun. He enjoys the camaraderie of working with his sales colleagues. He competes with them and himself. He makes customers like Ted happy. Yes, sales can be fun!

What Is Tough About a Sales Job?

Now that you've seen what's great about a career in sales, we'll discuss some of the less-than-optimal aspects of sales careers. These are the variables people don't often consider when thinking about a career in sales. Even successful sales professionals have difficulty with some of these variables from time to time.

Performance Is Required

That's right. Companies count on their salespeople to bring in more sales every year. Achieving objectives is the sales manager's and salesperson's responsibility. It is part of the job description. In a sales job, you might be asked not only to increase sales, but to meet certain profit standards as well. Salespeople cannot just pretend to work. Nothing will get sold and they will be out of a job. Whereas many office jobs will accommodate someone who is mediocre, sales will not. In most other professions, you are not given a performance review every four weeks. On a monthly basis, your boss doesn't analyze how many words you typed or how many tasks of a project you completed with 100 percent perfection. In sales, you are constantly on the scoreboard. Either you have made your sales objectives or you haven't. Every week and every month, the sales score is like a review. There is a sense of urgency in most sales jobs. Salespeople expect this and actually enjoy it.

The commission, or bonus dollars, you get paid is another report card. If you don't do well, it shows up as less money in your bank account.

You will notice this and so will your spouse. When you do a good job and bring in the bucks, it is a very satisfying feeling. Why? Because the flip side of this subject is that you really do get paid for your efforts. You could be the hardest working, most effective manager in an office and get paid the same salary as a lackluster peer. In time, however, your hard work would most likely pay off. On the other hand, if you are an effective, hard-working salesperson, you could make thousands of dollars more than the average salesperson at your company. In this case, the reward for your efforts is immediate.

Self-Management

Self-management is not as easy as it sounds. It doesn't mean freedom. What it really means is that you have to be effective with very little direction from a manager. For an Avon representative, it means making a plan on Friday afternoon for the next week. On Monday, she has to get out of bed, get organized, get the family on its way, and be at her desk making phone calls by a certain time. Nobody is going to walk up to her and say, "Here are your sales appointments for the week." She has to make follow-up calls to customers to see whether they have run out of a particular item. She must promote new items by bringing them to the attention of her customers and prospects who haven't yet purchased anything from her. All this must be done without allowing herself to be distracted by the tempting little chores she could be doing around the house.

A car salesperson has to make the follow-up calls to the prospects that came in that day and the day before. Nobody is going to do this for him. A stockbroker knows that she might have to make 50 calls per day, every day, to slowly build a client base. The same stockbroker will know that she will be turned down 45 times every day. Despite rejection (see the next section for more on this negative aspect of sales), these salespeople have to press on. They have to make the calls on the phone and in person. They have to have a plan for the week and the month. Real pros have a game plan for the year. They can tell you how many sales calls they need to make every day to be successful in their industry. This takes determination and good self-management.

Sales managers, sales trainers, and your sales colleagues will be available to help you. They will teach you, work with you, and advise you on how to improve your sales. But they won't be with you every minute of every day. Ultimately, you must manage and motivate yourself.

Rejection

Rejection is one of the first things people think of when considering sales. It is a big psychological issue. Nobody likes to be told "No."

"No, we don't have time to talk to you."

"No, we aren't interested."

"No, I can't schedule an appointment for you."

"No, we don't need your product."

"No, Mr. Curmudgeon doesn't see salespeople."

"Can't you see the sign? It says, 'No solicitors!'"

To succeed in sales you have to be confident enough of who you are to overcome the negatives. You need a "thick skin" to deflect the hurtful things people can and will say to you. Salespeople are easy targets for frustrated receptionists, secretaries, purchasing agents, small-business owners, office managers, doctors, and others who are a company's "first line of defense." If they are having a bad day, a salesperson makes the perfect punching bag.

You must learn to be somewhat forgiving of these people. Many times they don't mean what they say or do. They might have had an argument with a loved one the night before, or their boss might have just chewed them out. Perhaps they are just plain selfish. In a doctor's office full of patients, an unscheduled salesperson means that the staff might go home late. A nurse in such an office, where the doctor is already behind schedule, will not be terribly excited about seeing a salesperson. There are, however, very good methods for handling many of these situations, if the salesperson is willing to learn.

Working Alone

Working alone is a situation faced mostly by outside salespeople. It's lonely. The warm, fuzzy office environment they were accustomed to is gone. Look at the change a hospital nurse might face if he is changing to a medical-products or pharmaceutical sales job. As a nurse, he arrived at the hospital every day to the same people he had worked with for several months or many years. These people knew his family and friends. They complimented him on his haircut. They asked him about his weekend or vacation. They listened to his problems and pitched in to help when times were difficult (just as he did for them). They brought in a cake for his birthday and sang to him. You get the picture. There is a secure feeling built into this work environment. That feeling stops in outside sales.

Inside sales jobs frequently have more supportive environments just because you are in close proximity to your coworkers. This provides a sense of security. Advice and encouragement from a colleague or manager are just around the corner. Car dealerships and furniture stores are examples of inside sales businesses. Real-estate sales is a combination of inside and outside sales. An agent will work outside for much of the time but will go to the main office for advice, support, sales meetings, and so on. The salespeople in inside sales situations tend to support each other. For this reason, inside positions can be a very good first step into sales.

Risk-Reward Compensation

By accepting a sales compensation plan, you are agreeing to a risk-reward proposition. You are accepting a small base salary, or perhaps none at all. At the same time, you have access to a commission/bonus plan that might double or triple your salary. You have to be willing to take the risk that you will be able to meet your sales objectives and earn your commission. If you meet or exceed your sales objectives, you will be rewarded with substantial commission checks. You might also win an award and a trip for you and a companion. If you don't meet your objectives, you might have to tighten the budget belt at home because your commissions will be significantly lower. There might also be a ramp-up period in income while you build sales volume and commissions. This might mean that you make less money for a month or two. Some people think this is just too risky. They would rather have a job that pays a steady amount of money regardless of what good or bad fortunes their company is experiencing.

Competition

Wait a minute. Didn't we just say competition was one of the great things about sales? Yes, it is, but it can be a double-edged sword, serving as both a positive driving force and a source of stress. Competition does require a thick skin. To compete in sales means that sometimes you are going to win and sometimes you are going to lose. You might lose a customer. You might not succeed in convincing a potential customer to buy your product or service. You might not make your sales goal one month or one year. After working hard all year toward the goals of a sales contest, you might fall short of qualifying for the prize. You must be able to handle the inevitable ups and downs of a competitive environment. Most salespeople find this atmosphere very stimulating and fun. True professionals find a way to bounce back from a losing experience and go for a win. In fact, many are re-motivated by the "loss."

Bad Management

Bad management can break a budding salesperson. It always pains us to hear the discouraged voice of someone who has been poorly managed. In your eagerness to find a sales position, it is important that you also find a good manager. A good manager can be encouraging and supportive while at the same time pressuring you to get results. Don't confuse positive pressure with bad management. Sales managers are expected to challenge you. They are like sports coaches. You might curse them in the middle of the year when they are pushing you and asking you to try some different approaches. But at the end of the year (like the end of the game), when you have overachieved your objectives, you might feel like hugging that manager.

On the other hand, there are some bad managers. They tend to rule their salespeople with force and through fear. You don't want to work for them. If you find yourself in such an environment, you must get out before you let that manager demoralize you, ruin your self-esteem, and damage your career.

Sales Levels and Plateaus

Sales levels and plateaus can be intimidating to the new salesperson. Some salespeople take over another salesperson's territory, where a level of sales already exists. The management of the company expects that level to be exceeded. Others might start at zero sales. For example, a new Weekenders or Amway salesperson will start from scratch.

In all these cases, the most intimidating factor is to make the first sale! Ted remembers his first sale. Even though he took over an existing territory, it wasn't until he made the first sale that he started to gain momentum. Faith is required here!

- Faith that you have a good product.

- Faith that you have good support.

- Faith that you have been trained properly so that you can clearly discuss your products and services with customers.

Remember when you learned something difficult or scary? Good examples are learning to swim or ride a bike. Most likely your parents were telling you, "You can do it! Pedal hard and the bike will stay up!" Or, "Jump in and swim to me! You don't need my help anymore. The last time I helped you, you did it all by yourself! You can do it!" When you finally pedaled the bike or took the plunge, you finished with a smile on your face and the thought, "That wasn't so hard. Gee, I am good!" Now many of you are reliving this experience with your own children. And in the process, you are constantly thinking to yourself, "If he would only listen and do what I say. He is so close to swimming properly!"

Sales is not a lot different. It is learning something new. If you are entering sales as a full-time career or a part-time effort to make more money, you must give yourself a chance to get your first sale. You must listen to the people saying, "You can do it!" You must have faith in the guidance you receive from experienced and successful managers and mentors. Then you must be willing to work through the first sales plateau.

A *sales plateau* is the first level of consistent sales revenue that you reach. It is directly related to a combination of your sales traits and skills (which are discussed in chapter 5). Some people get frustrated when they feel they are stuck on a sales plateau for a period of time. They feel like they are failing because they are not progressing more swiftly. Again, effort backed by faith is required here. The new salesperson must keep learning and practicing. If she persists, she will break out of the plateau and move up to a higher sales plateau, where the cycle of learning and practicing will begin again. Our advice to those who take the plunge into a career in sales is to learn, listen, and persist. You will probably surprise yourself in a very positive way.

Wrap-up and To Do

Now what is going through your mind? If you've read this chapter and continue to have enthusiasm for the idea of a sales career, you might have some of that "thick skin" we mentioned. That's good. If the "tough" part of the chapter creates some anxiety, you might not be cut out for this career.

In either case, we recommend that you take the points in this chapter and discuss them with two or three people you know who have a sales or sales-management job. Get their perspective. Be sure you talk specifically about your concerns, and see if you get concrete ideas for ways you can be successful when you meet challenges in sales. Ask your contacts how they overcame the obstacles in their various sales positions.

Don't be afraid to challenge yourself, but do get a realistic idea of what kinds of obstacles you'll face. If you decide to go ahead and pursue a sales career, you'll be better prepared when the tough times occur and will be able to look forward to the peaks.

CHAPTER 3 A Week in the Life of a Sales Professional

You are learning that the career of a salesperson is very interesting yet very different from many other careers. But what is the life really like—day to day, week to week? In this chapter, we take a detailed look at a week in the life of three salespeople. These are real people. Like you, there was a time when they wondered what they were going to do as a career. They chose sales. The roles they are in right now are advanced, but they started on the low end of the sales ladder and worked their way into the positions they have today. As we follow Bud, Peirce, and Kathy through a week, you will see a number of important personality traits and sales skills that are key to selling success. Traits and skills are discussed in detail in chapter 5. In this chapter, you'll get a vivid preview of why these traits are important in the life of a salesperson.

A Week with Bud Zuberer, Senior Automation Consultant for a Leading Pharmacy Automation Company

It is late Sunday evening and Bud is at Tampa International Airport waiting for a flight to Atlanta. Bud spends an average of three and a half days each week on the road and only a day and a half in his office. He works out of his home. His office is a well-organized room above his garage.

Bud sells robots. Not the robots of science fiction. Not cyborgs with arms and legs that walk and talk. He sells machines that automate the process of picking and dispensing medications in hospitals. If you have been in a hospital lately, you might have seen one on one of the floors, but you probably didn't know that the large gray cabinet was a virtual pharmacy taking care of the needs of the patients on the floor. These automation systems can save hospitals tens of thousands of dollars annually. They also reduce the incidence of wrong prescriptions being given to patients.

Monday

Monday, in Georgia, Bud will be assisting another automation consultant. They will be meeting with a customer to get the customer's agreement for an important part of the sales process—the customer's commitment to perform a study to evaluate the potential benefits of utilizing an automated-pharmacy system. Two things are going on here. First, Bud is demonstrating team play. He is helping out a fellow sales representative who has not yet earned the "senior" title. Second, they are moving a potential customer through the sales process.

To get this far, they have already taken three important steps. The first step was a short phone call to a key contact at the hospital to confirm a real interest in automating some or all of the pharmacy functions. In that phone call an appointment was made for a second, hour-long phone call. During this second call, the automation consultant asked a lot of questions and listened intently to understand what the hospital expected automation to do for it. His colleague then visited the site to verify that the data collected during the phone meeting were correct. For this visit—stage three of this lengthy sales process—Bud and his co-worker arrive armed only with a pen, pad, and already-collected information. They will show no literature from the company nor push for a sale. The visit is intended as a broader fact-finding mission. The team confirms the information initially gathered and goes on to collect even more information. During this meeting, Bud also starts to promote the concept of conducting an in-depth study at the hospital to put a dollar figure on the financial benefits of becoming automated.

At the end of this face-to-face fact-finding mission, the hospital, Bud, and his fellow automation consultant agree to yet another meeting. This one will be face-to-face with the key hospital administrators. During this meeting, Bud will be armed with a detailed presentation that provides a broad overview of the technology and how it directly applies to this facility's goals and objectives. If Bud's company is to do an in-depth study with the hospital, it will need to invest a lot of resources and incur significant expenses. Bud and his colleague will want to be sure that the hospital is really committed to the potential purchase of a system. At this meeting, Bud will ask that several members of upper management, if not the entire "C suite" of the hospital, be present. The C-suite comprises the Chief Operating Officer, Chief Nursing Officer, Chief Financial Officer, CEO, and Head Pharmacist. These people would not get together for a meeting unless there was serious interest in Bud's products and services. At this meeting—the one Bud is leaving for as we start this story—Bud will be seeking agreement to do an in-depth study.

You can tell that this is a lengthy and detail-oriented process that requires good listening skills, relationship skills, and organizational skills. It also requires leadership abilities. In this case, Bud and his colleague are providing leadership to the hospital based on their expertise. Throughout the process they have gained the respect of the hospital staff—enough respect that they can ask for the meeting of the C-suite.

Tuesday

On Tuesday, Bud will be headed to New Orleans to do the same thing with a different automation consultant. Bud's territory is the northern half of Florida and New Orleans. It might seem odd to have New Orleans thrown in there. However, Bud happened to have strong contacts in New Orleans due to previous positions. The pharmacy-automation company recognized this strength and asked him to include the city in his territory.

When Bud makes a sale, it is usually somewhere between $1.5 million and $5 million. His annual sales last year were over $14 million. So, he sold somewhere between five and seven systems. His position is definitely in the category of capital equipment sales. Also, these sales have long selling cycles. It might take anywhere from six months to two years for a hospital to make the decision to buy one of his automation systems. When a hospital pays this much for a product, it will have staff involved at every level. This means that Bud will be interacting with everyone from the purchasing department through nursing through pharmacy and on up to the executive suite. He will also be involving a number of other people at his company—implementation teams, clinical support teams, financial departments, and architects. Bud has to be able to demonstrate leadership and an ability to work with a team to get the job done. This is not an entry-level sales position that you might get right out of college. So how did he get here?

After graduating from Duke, Bud started working in sales for Union Camp selling paper products. This was a grueling initiation to sales. He excelled and knew he had the potential to sell more sophisticated products for companies that would pay him more. Through some personal connections (his network), Bud knew of a cardiology products company named Zymed that was growing and hiring salespeople. He interviewed for the job and got the classic, "You're a great guy, but you have no experience with high-tech medical devices. We can't consider you seriously." Bud's trait of pure determination kicked into high gear. It was a trait that was born in a family of competitors and led to a four-year scholarship to play football at Duke. It is part of his competitive philosophy that rises to any challenge and never gives up. His response to the rejection was a challenge to his interviewers. He said, "I will make you a deal. If I can meet you again in three months and prove that I know as much or more about the heart and arrhythmia than you do, you will hire me." They agreed, probably thinking they would never hear from him again. Wrong. He stayed in contact and began lugging around a heavy stack of books about the heart. Three months later, Bud proved his point, and Zymed offered Bud the job he had studied so hard for. Then, in his first year as a Zymed representative, he outsold all the other reps at the company.

From Zymed he was hired by Johnson & Johnson to sell sterilization equipment to hospitals. This was Bud's first experience with larger capital equipment and a step up on his career path. He gained expertise that positioned him for a role with his current company's more sophisticated and expensive capital equipment. With the pharmacy-automation company, Bud has always been one of the top five sales consultants.

Wednesday

On Wednesday, he will be back in his home office. This will be a busy day of phone calls. His philosophy is that he doesn't want to spend time doing paperwork during hours in which he can be in contact with prospects, customers, or company teammates. Here's what Bud's phone schedule for Wednesday looks like:

- Calling prospects to determine their level of interest in the products and services he has to offer. If they are not immediately interested, he will set a time to call back in the next six months to a year.

- Two hour-long fact-finding calls with a prospect hospital that has shown interest in automation.

- Numerous calls to his teammates. He might update his regional manager on his various sales projects. He will confer with different members of his implementation teams to review their progress.

- Quick call to the automation consultant he is mentoring.

- Calls to schedule future fact-finding meetings with some customers and final-sale negotiations with other customers.

The day will be a blur. Between calls, he will answer and compose e-mails to customers and teammates. That night, perhaps after the kids are in bed, Bud will do his paperwork, expense reports, and project reports. He might also work on a computerized presentation he plans on making to a hospital's C-suite.

Thursday

Thursday, Bud heads for Jacksonville, Florida, to conduct a first face-to-face fact-finding session at a military hospital.

Friday

Friday, he will remain in Jacksonville to meet with a hospital that has purchased his company's automation system. This is a follow-up meeting on a special project with the hospital. The company and the hospital are doing the statistical research on how the automation has benefited the hospital financially. Both the company and the hospital are eager to quantify the value of the automation. The hospital might influence others in its chain to do the same. Bud and his colleagues will be able to use the data to prove to other prospective hospitals that they have something very valuable to offer.

Just by seeing how Bud Zuberer conducts his work throughout a week tells you that he is passionate about his job and his products. He has worked hard along a progressive career path. He has the psychic reward of dealing with high-level managers in the health-care industry. These hospital executives occasionally move to other hospitals. By maintaining these relationships, Bud frequently finds that new doors open for him. With self-discipline he drives himself hard throughout the week. He optimizes his time. Finally, he is part of the spirit of a tightly knit group of automation specialists and implementation specialists with whom he really enjoys working. If he were ever to have a rough day, he has teammates ready to pump him back up. Bud is the definition of a professional salesperson. The reward for his discipline, passion, determination, and hard work is a very healthy income in the top tier of medical-product sales.

A Week with Peirce Ward, New England Financial Network

Peirce is in the business of protecting people, families, and businesses from the consequences of death and disability. He also helps people assure themselves of a comfortable retirement. Most of his sales are in the form of life insurance, annuities, long-term care, and retirement plans. It sounds like plain old insurance sales. This is far from the truth. Unlike the simple and manipulative ads for inexpensive life insurance we get in the mail and see on TV, the New England Financial Network offers a variety of forms of sophisticated and high-quality life insurance. The "quality" comes in the way the insurance, annuity, or care contract is written and the way it is positioned to the covered person and his or her beneficiaries. To recommend the right products and the right positioning, Peirce has had to develop a knowledge of people, finances, taxes, and estates.

Peirce is a success in his industry. He always qualifies for the Million Dollar Round Table, which puts him in the top 4 percent of life-insurance professionals in the country. This year he will qualify for the Court of the Table, the top 2 percent of insurance professionals. He got to this level through hard work. It wasn't easy.

After graduating with an MBA from Rollins College in Winter Park, Florida, Peirce entered a Bank of America training program. He started as a credit analyst in the loan department. Then, in a move that would nudge him toward sales, he became a regional marketing manager for the bank. All along, people were telling him that he would be good in sales because of his outgoing, can-do personality. At the same time, he was seeing the limitations of a banking career from the standpoint of personal financial growth. He also frequently reflected on his father's career. It was an endless string of long commutes to work in New York City and a life run by a corporation. One day, one of Peirce's banking colleagues suggested that he try life-insurance sales.

Some people think that insurance companies will take anyone for sales jobs. Not true. The top companies are careful in their selection. These companies have worked hard to develop a reputation for superb products and top-notch people to represent these products. They also invest a lot of time and money in their agents. The New England Financial Network is one of the top companies in the industry. When Peirce approached them about a job as an agent, they asked him to take a battery of tests. After the results of the tests were available, he sat down with the general agent to discuss whether or not he should make this career move. The tests were positive and the general agent encouraged Peirce to proceed. He also offered Peirce income in the form of a draw against commission to help him get started.

Monday

It is 8:00 a.m. and Peirce has already been at his desk for some time reviewing his schedule for the week. He has a staff of two people who help him optimize his time. Today is a "focus" day. Wednesday and Friday will be focus days, too. Tuesday and Thursday will be "buffer" days. Focus days are for selling. High-level financial presentations take a lot of energy. Whether he's meeting a client for lunch or making a presentation to the estate-planning team for a wealthy businesswoman, it is showtime. Buffer days are for phone work, getting all the supportive paperwork done, getting reenergized, and preparing for the next day of high-level meetings.

At 9:00 a.m. Peirce's coach will call. Peirce has hired a strategic coach to help him stay on track with his business and personal goals. After the coaching session, it will be a day of meetings with clients and prospective clients.

It is 11:45 a.m. and Peirce is in a Charlotte restaurant sitting across the table from a prospective client. This luncheon appointment is the culmination of a dozen phone calls and one previously cancelled lunch. It wasn't easy. This prospect came to Peirce's attention through another satisfied and long-term client. Sometimes, on a focus day, Peirce might meet with one of his clients for a brief review of their insurance programs. It is at this time that he might ask them for a referral. Asking for referrals is an important part of finding new clients. Peirce has known some of his clients for years and has their confidence. They know that he will approach any referral professionally. This reputation of professionalism is an asset that Peirce has worked hard to develop. The prospect he is having lunch with respects the other person who gave Peirce his name. This opening creates the framework for a constructive discussion over lunch.

At a first meeting like this, Peirce is trying to accomplish several things. First, he is demonstrating his professionalism and knowledge of his product. Second, he is trying to get to know enough about this prospect to get a general sense of what insurance products might be useful. This is called fact-finding. Finally, through good fact-finding, he is winning the prospect's trust. Peirce has not brought any brochures or other company literature. He is carrying only a small notepad and a pen. Over lunch, Peirce is trying to sell himself and the need for another meeting in which the prospect can share more detailed information. Only then can Peirce begin to clearly picture the exact insurance products that will benefit the prospect most.

The second appointment of the day is at 4:00 p.m. at the office of an executive of a local distribution company. At this second meeting with a new prospective client, Peirce will present two possible insurance plans. This woman isn't a client…yet. She has asked her estate attorney to join in the meeting. In fact, it was the estate attorney who knew of Peirce and suggested that she contact him. This is a nice referral.

Referrals didn't come easily for Peirce when he started at New England. He had to make a lot of cold calls on the phone to get many of his first customers. He followed the scientific formula of a large number of calls resulting in a small number of sales. It was hard work. He frequently wondered what the heck he was doing. At the same time, he was determined to figure out how to be successful at insurance sales. In his office there were several seasoned agents who were very successful and making good money. Meanwhile, Peirce was thankful that his wife had a job.

Now it is different. He gets referrals. His persistence has paid off. He jokes that when he started in the business, his friends thought he was crazy for taking such a risky job. However, insurance commissions are paid out over a number of years. Today, Peirce is getting paid commissions not only on current sales, but also some commissions on the sales he's made over the past 10 years. This means that he has created a kind of security in consistent income. Now Peirce isn't the one at risk for job security. However, some of those same friends who thought he was crazy are living in a world of corporate downsizing and bankruptcy.

Although Monday was productive, the fact that he had only two face-to-face meetings with clients disturbs Peirce. His goal is three in-person appointments on focus days or nine per week on average. He knows that if he achieves this number with well-qualified prospects and clients, he will achieve the sales goals that he has set for himself. He makes a mental note to try to fit four meetings into a focus day in the near future. When setting up meetings, Peirce's marketing assistant tries to set them on the hour and provide for at least an hour in between.

Tuesday

Tuesday is a buffer day. Peirce meets with his policy-service administrator several times during the day. She is helping him prepare for upcoming meetings with current clients. For example, she might be pulling together an update on the client's policies so that he and the client can conduct an annual review. She will also be working with Peirce to stay on top of the status of the various insurance applications that have been submitted. Perhaps she is helping to arrange for a physical exam for a prospect or client.

He also has a marketing assistant. It is her job to help process referrals and other leads that need to be turned into appointments. She will also assist him in preparing slides and proposal binders. When he finally makes a first presentation of an insurance plan, he is usually armed with computerized slides and a binder that is custom made for the prospect.

Wednesday

Wednesday is a busy day. First Peirce meets over coffee with a prospect, then holds an annual review for a client over lunch, and finally delivers a fairly basic final presentation in the afternoon to a young married couple. It ends up being a great day. The prospect wants to move forward with another meeting. The annual review resulted in an instant sale of a $150,000 variable life policy. Peirce knew this successful client needed to bolster his insurance program. However, he was surprised when the client suggested the additional policy before he did. Finally, the young couple agreed that they both needed to start an insurance program. At Peirce's suggestion, they started with a package of term and variable life for a total of $100,000 each. In sales, some days are like this. When you work hard, prepare diligently, maintain faith in yourself, and keep a smile on your face, amazing things can happen. Days like this more than make up for the more difficult ones.

Thursday

It's Thursday and another buffer day. Peirce and his team are busy processing the applications on the insurance they sold the day before, finalizing a presentation for Friday, confirming appointments for the following week, setting up appointments with referrals two and three weeks out, and working on a newsletter to clients.

Friday

Friday is a three-appointment day. The morning appointment is with a small-business owner in his mid 30s. After 45 minutes of conversation and general fact-finding, Peirce determines that this fellow isn't really serious about protecting his family or putting money away for college education and retirement. Peirce politely cuts the meeting short and offers to call the man back in a year. The lunch appointment is another annual review of policies with a current client who is well respected in business circles in Charlotte. Although this lunch won't result in a sale in the near future, it does result in four really good referrals. This is the first time this client has referred friends and colleagues to Peirce. For Peirce, it is as good as a sale. The 3:00 p.m. meeting is a good initial meeting with a serious young newlywed optometrist who insists on moving right into fact-finding so that Peirce can get a proposal to him the next week. This is a great way to finish a very productive week.

In this week with Peirce Ward, you have seen a man working for himself under the umbrella of a well-respected insurance company. In this type of sales position, Peirce is his own boss. He has no quotas set by New England Financial Network or a sales manager. He sets his own objectives and pursues them diligently. He demonstrates discipline, leadership, excellent salesmanship, good organizational skills, and many more of the traits and skills we have identified as being important for success in sales.

A Week with Kathy T.—from Teacher to Sales Manager

Kathy remembers how it all started for her. After receiving her master's degree and a certification in art education, Kathy began teaching art. She liked teaching. She liked art. And she was good at both. Some summers, at art fairs, she would sell jewelry that she had created. Despite her success at art and teaching, she felt a couple of things were missing. One of those things was getting recognition for a job well done, recognition that teachers don't often receive. Then there was the issue of money. It's no secret that teachers don't make a lot of money despite the fact that they are some of the best-educated people in the workforce.

Kathy's first exposure to sales came with a nationally known direct-sales cosmetics company. For a short period of time, Kathy sold this excellent product line part-time. Cosmetics didn't fit her selling personality, so she decided not to represent the line. However, she was exposed to the upbeat and progressive nature of a well-run direct-sales organization. She liked the other women in the organization. She liked the recognition she saw given out every week. This experience was fertilizer sprinkled on a seed in her mind. And Kathy kept on teaching.

A couple years later, Kathy was invited to a friend's home for a presentation of fashionable yet easy-care clothing. One of her fellow teachers was the fashion consultant. She liked the clothing that was presented and purchased some. That was nine years ago.

A little over seven years ago, Kathy became a fashion consultant for the same company. It wasn't a difficult decision. "I loved the clothes and the art of fashion. How difficult could this be?" She began her sales career part-time while she continued to teach. The clothing line fit her selling personality. So did the other women she worked with. Seven years ago, this direct-sales clothing company had about 3,000 fashion consultants in North America. Now there are over 15,000 women across America selling this popular upscale, easy-care clothing line part-time and full-time. The company provides a supportive and enthusiastic environment that recognizes individuals for their accomplishments. Kathy had found her place. When asked about the move from teaching to sales she responded, "Teachers are selling education and ideas to children, and moms are selling broccoli to their kids." To her, it wasn't that big a paradigm shift. The supportive nature of the company was also a big factor in making the move.

Saturday

On this Saturday, Kathy is greeted at the door by Ann, a tall woman with a warm smile. Once inside, the Milwaukee winter chill is dispelled by the pleasant aroma of coffee. Ann is hosting this get-together. Right behind Kathy arrives JoAnn, one of Kathy's novice fashion consultants. She thanks Kathy quietly and profusely for coming to assist her with her first group presentation of clothing. Kathy can see that JoAnn is both nervous and excited. As JoAnn's sponsor, Kathy is also her sales manager. The two women get everything in order and discuss the agenda one more time as Ann welcomes the last of the five invited guests.

The Saturday-afternoon presentation goes well. JoAnn can hardly believe it. Her first event nets $600 of purchases. Kathy remembers her first presentation, over seven years ago, when she earned $500. Now, Kathy coaches JoAnn on the proper follow-up procedure to thank the women for coming and becoming customers. She also helps JoAnn with the paperwork to submit the various orders. Finally, Kathy gives advice on how JoAnn can take the positive momentum of her first presentation and turn it into other hosted presentations.

Presentations can be to a group of women in the home of a host. Or, a presentation can be made for an individual. A "hostess" is a woman who agrees to invite some friends to a showing in her home. The hostess earns free clothing and accessories.

As a Sales Manager, Kathy has more than 20 fashion consultants working with her. These are all women whom she has "sponsored." Most are part-time and some are full time. A few of these consultants have started sponsoring more women. Some of Kathy's week is spent doing management work for her team. The other part of her week is spent organizing her own presentations for her customer base. Notice that we say that the other fashion consultants are "working with" Kathy. We don't say "working for." That is partly the "women working with women" philosophy of the company. It is also partly a fact of life. These women have asked Kathy to sponsor them. They are all in business for themselves. Kathy's role is to provide them with a healthy, upbeat, instructive, and productive environment within which to succeed. She doesn't feel like a "boss."

Most presentations are scheduled for evenings and weekends, and evenings are Kathy's most productive contact and presentation time. Her days are spent doing follow-up work.

Monday

This Monday Kathy will be hard at work organizing her monthly team meeting. These meetings consist of the following:

- Product training on new and current products
- Selling tips
- Sharing of success stories—such as JoAnn's first successful presentation

- Recognizing team members for new goals reached, sales, and other achievements

- A warm welcome to newly sponsored fashion consultants

- Preparation for the national pre-spring company show

She will get the agenda out by e-mail and make calls to remind her team of the date.

Kathy has worked her way up into the Sales Manager role. There is a specific path one follows to do this. As mentioned earlier, she started out part-time. In 1998, she resigned from teaching and went full-time with the company. When she had sponsored three other women, she became a team leader. Finally, when she hit the magic number of 20 sponsored fashion consultants, she earned the first prestigious title of Sales Manager.

Monday evening she puts a call in to a woman who is hosting a presentation for the first time this Thursday evening. This woman has been a customer for over a year. To help her out, Kathy has her think back to the presentations she has attended at another person's home. The objective is to have five to eight women attend. She should make a call to remind the invitees and be ready to tell them what she likes about the clothes she has purchased. The refreshments should be kept simple, Kathy tells her. Kathy also reminds her that these gatherings are intended to be fun. The customer is glad Kathy called and sounds more confident about the coming event.

Tuesday

Tuesday a package from the company arrives with the details of the February spring/summer fashion conference. There are two of these conferences per year at which the new seasonal clothes are introduced. The programs are wonderful events where managers and consultants are recognized for their achievements and product training is provided for the new fashions. Kathy will strongly encourage the members of her team to attend; however, it is not mandatory. Kathy will bring news back from the meeting and deliver the appropriate training to her team. However, she knows how motivating these meetings can be. She knows what it is like to be recognized for an achievement and hear the roar of approval and the applause from thousands of other women. She would love for more members of her team to experience this.

As a Sales Manager, Kathy's expenses for these two national conferences are paid for by the company. This is unusual in the direct-sales industry. In addition to these two national conferences, Kathy is invited to three other managers' meetings per year. These three meetings are for Sales Managers, Senior Sales Managers, Executives, and Senior Executives. The focus is on sales management and leadership. At these meetings, Kathy will rub shoulders with the executive management of the dynamic company. She might even find herself in a session with the founders of the company. These trips are also paid for by the company.

Tuesday evening Kathy has a very successful presentation. It is the third time this hostess has had a presentation. A number of the women are already customers. It is not hard for her to create a very credible atmosphere and sell over $1,500 worth of clothing. In addition, the hostess agrees to and announces a date for the next presentation, when Kathy will bring in the new spring/summer line of clothes. Kathy has another big plus this evening: One of the women takes Kathy aside and inquires about being a fashion consultant. For Kathy it has always seemed this easy. "I don't feel like I am selling anything," she says. "I share information about great products and the customers make their own decisions." The result is that Kathy makes far more money than she did as a teacher in fewer hours per week and with less stress.

This business is seasonal. March, April, and May are the busiest months because of the introduction of seasonal fashions. During this period, Kathy averages three presentations per week. In July and August she might have one presentation per week. Then in the fall, from September through November, she will get busy again. Due to the size of her customer base, Kathy will often take individual orders over the phone. Between seasons there is a lot of follow-up work to be done.

Wednesday

During the day on Wednesday, Kathy will spend most of her time on personal activities such as household chores, shopping, and exercise. When planning her week, she intentionally sets aside this time. She is the master of her schedule. She is her own boss. No one is looking over her shoulder critiquing her work. Kathy seems to have the natural discipline to put the time into being successful and find time for herself. This evening she has set aside for phone calls to some of her customers to see if they need anything and to find willing hostesses for future presentations. She will also call the new hostess of Thursday evening's presentation to see if there are any last-minute questions.

Thursday

Thursday, Kathy begins working on her monthly newsletter. She also catches up on her mail. A few calls come in from newer consultants on her team with questions about product features and paperwork. Another consultant calls to get Kathy's advice about going full-time. And she receives a commission check from the company. This always brings a smile to her face. She receives commissions from her direct sales and a percentage of the sales of the women in her team.

Thursday evening, Kathy has the presentation. Her hostess does a good job. Five women, all new to the company, attend. Three of the women purchase clothing for a total of $800. This is a good start for this new group and Kathy is pleased with the outcome.

Friday

On Friday, Kathy wraps up the week by placing orders, making some phone calls, planning her travel to the national spring/summer conference, and following up on other paperwork. She looks back on the week with a lot of satisfaction. It was a busier-than-normal off-season week. One of the best moments of the week was the excited call from one of the part-time consultants who had just received her largest commission check ever. One of her experienced full-time consultants has begun building her own network of consultants and is making over $40,000 per year. Most of Kathy's part-time consultants easily make $4,000 to $5,000 per year. This money goes to college funds, vacations, retirement funds, and remodeling projects. It makes a big difference to the families of these consultants. In addition to that, Kathy, with the help of the company, created a motivating environment in which to earn these extra dollars. What more could she want? Nothing. She loves her sales career.

Wrap-up and To Do

In this chapter, you've had the chance to peek into the lives of three successful sales professionals. These three individuals sell very different products to very different customers, but similar themes emerge: They all believe in what they're selling. They all put a lot of time and effort into their jobs. They combine face-to-face sales (the image many people see when they think of a sales career) with all-important planning and behind-the-scenes preparation.

What do you think? Would this kind of life be satisfying for you, and is it a good fit for your traits, abilities, and interests? These stories can help you better define your career goal and the kinds of companies and products you'd like to represent.

CHAPTER 4　What Does a Sales Job Pay?

The way salespeople are paid is very different from the way people are paid for other lines of work. As discussed in chapter 2, this can be a tremendous advantage and at the same time it can be very intimidating. For the most part, people in non-sales positions are paid an hourly wage or annual salary. They know exactly what their paycheck is going to look like every two weeks. This is comforting and predictable, and makes it easy to budget living expenses, savings and investments, vacations, and so forth. A salesperson's paycheck can be very different from one period to the next. For someone new to sales, this can be nerve-racking. But the experienced salesperson wouldn't have it any other way!

A clear understanding of how sales compensation works is important for two reasons. First, it will help you better understand how a move into sales can affect you financially. Second, it will help you intelligently discuss compensation with a potential employer. Before you start interviewing, we also strongly suggest that you arm yourself with the latest information on average salaries for the industries, companies, and geographic regions you're targeting. You can do this by using Internet-based salary-comparison tools, gleaning compensation information from online and print job postings, and searching the Internet for salary-survey information. In the appendix, we list some resources for finding this information.

Sales Compensation Overview

Sales compensation can be made up of a number of components. Most sales jobs are a combination of a steady base salary and monthly commissions, along with other variables. Exactly what these components are and how they work together can be quite different from one job or industry to another. The following sections look closely at each of the possible components of a salesperson's compensation: commission, salary, car allowance, bonuses, awards, stock awards, and stock options.

Commission

In most sales positions, commissions are the most important part of compensation. It is commissions that make selling so financially rewarding. A commission is a percentage of the price of a product/ service that is paid to the salesperson who sold it. For example, let's say a company pays a 5 percent commission for every $200 widget that is sold. That means a salesperson gets $10 every time he or she sells a widget. Sales of $20,000 worth of widgets in one month would equal $1,000 in commissions.

Understanding Sales Quotas

So that you can better understand commissions, we must first talk about quotas, budgets, and sales goals. All of these terms essentially mean the same thing. A *sales quota* is the sales goal the company assigns to the salesperson. It is not only a goal; it is also an expectation. The quota is usually a certain dollar amount for the period of a year. Then it is broken down into quarters and months. Sales specialists at one of the companies Ted worked for had annual quotas of $1,000,000. This was then broken down into months. Because the product was seasonal, sales were always higher in certain months of the year than in others. This seasonality was built into the monthly quotas. For example, it was possible that the June sales quota would be higher than the quota for July.

Of course, most companies are in the business of growing. That translates into increased quotas every year. Many companies work with their salespeople to help determine what the quotas for the next year should be. This is called *bottom-up forecasting.* So although the idea of quotas might sound intimidating, in some cases you might have input about your future sales expectations.

Most home-based selling environments such as Mary Kay and Amway do not have quotas, although you might have to achieve a minimum level of sales before you begin recruiting others to join your sales team. In these businesses, when you sell their products you are acting as a *distributor.* In effect, you are in business for yourself representing their product. It is up to you to set your own goals and quotas.

How Commissions Are Paid

Typically, commissions are paid on a monthly basis. They are the carrot dangling in front of the salesperson. Often commissions are tied to a monthly goal. For example, the goal might be to sell $20,000 worth of widgets per month. If 100 percent of the goal is reached—in other words, $20,000 of widgets are sold—the salesperson might get a 5 percent commission, earning $1,000 in commission income that month. If the salesperson doesn't reach the goal for the month, the percentage of the commission might be lower. In the case of the widgets, it could be 4 percent. Let's say the salesperson sold $19,000 of widgets. Instead of close to $1,000 in income, he would receive only $760 under this structure. On the other hand, if the salesperson has a great month and overachieves the goal by $5,000, the company might reward this effort by paying a 7 percent commission on all these incremental sales (sales above the quota). This is sometimes called an *incremental commission structure.* The salesperson is motivated every month to sell as many widgets as possible. In this instance, the salesperson would be rewarded for this extraordinary effort by an extra $350 in his paycheck (7 percent on the incremental $5,000). The commission structure provides a company with a consistent flow of revenue.

How Commissions Are Structured

Commissions can vary widely from one industry to another and between companies in the same industry. The reasons for the differences are related to the nature of the product/service and the complexity of the sale. Complex sales require a higher level of selling skills. As you can imagine, the commissions paid for selling a newspaper subscription are much lower than those paid to the sales specialist of a company selling mainframe computers.

Yet commissions can also vary within an industry. Let's take automobiles as an example. A Kia dealer might have to pay a higher commission than a Ford dealer. Why? Because even salespeople can become averse to risks. Experienced car salespeople might consider Kia to be a risky selling situation. It is relatively new in the marketplace. Will the company survive after several years? Why leave a good job selling Fords or Toyotas? One way the Kia dealer can get these salespeople to take the risk of changing dealerships is to offer a higher commission.

Commissions can be very simple or very complicated. A company might pay a straight commission on the sales of all products all year long. Another company might pay different commissions on different products or at different times. The reason for the difference could be related to the profitability of a product or a specific company goal. If one product is more profitable than others, the company might be willing to pay a higher commission on it. It only makes sense that the more high-profit products a company sells, the better off everyone will be. Or let's say a company is launching a new product. To get the salespeople to pay more attention to this new product, the company might pay a higher commission on it for a limited period of time.

Commissions can be paid on pure sales or on another target—profits, for example. Paying commissions on the profits of what they sell is a great way to get salespeople to concentrate on pricing the products in such a way as to assure the company's profitability. This prevents salespeople from discounting products recklessly.

Most companies use commission structure to motivate salespeople to reach for certain goals. Several paragraphs ago we described an incremental program. A *graduated commission structure* is different from that, yet is still very motivating. For example, a company could pay 5 percent commission on the first 30 units a salesperson sells. Then it could pay 7 percent on the sales of units 31 to 40, and 10 percent on the sales of units 41 to 50. Obviously, salespeople see this structure and are motivated to sell the first 30 units as quickly as possible so that they can get into the higher commission brackets. Perhaps it takes four or six months to sell the first 30 units. From then on the commission is higher. This commission program is occasionally used in high-priced capital equipment sales.

Commission Only

In some industries the entire compensation package may be commission only. That means there is no salary. Although this seems scary, successful salespeople in these situations frequently make a lot of money. This is an example of the risk-to-reward ratio in action: The risk is higher, but so is the possible reward. Most part-time, home-based selling situations are commission only. For example, Amway distributors are paid only commissions on the products they sell or those that their networks sell.

Commissions can fluctuate widely from month to month depending on what has been sold. A salesperson could have one very good month of sales followed by a poor month. The result will be a high commission check followed by a low commission check. Of course, the whole idea of sales is to have more good months than bad. In capital equipment sales, a salesperson might go months between commission checks. However, those checks could be very big.

You might think that this type of compensation is too unpredictable, and in fact it is another of the risks of sales as a career. Of course, with every risk there is the chance of reward. The reward for the hard-working and effective salesperson is a consistently high level of income.

Draw Against Commission

Have you ever heard of a "draw against commission"? As mentioned earlier, a 100 percent commission compensation program can seem very intimidating. To reduce the stress of working on pure commissions, some companies offer a *draw,* which is a set amount of money on a monthly basis. The minute you make a sale and earn a commission, your commission dollars are applied against the draw that you have been paid. In a sense, it is like getting your commission paid up front. After a salesperson proves himself and is earning regular commission checks, the draw will diminish and eventually disappear, to be replaced by the straight sales commission. Some car dealers and some of the best insurance companies pay their salespeople a draw against commission.

Salary

Most full-time sales jobs have a salary as part of the total compensation plan. The amount of the salary is dependent on a number of factors including industry standards, the individual's level of experience, company strategies, and so forth. A salary gives the salesperson a measure of consistency and security. As discussed earlier, commissions might fluctuate from month to month. A salary helps moderate these fluctuations. In many sales positions that have a salary-and-commission structure, by meeting your sales goals you will earn commissions that equal your salary. Of course, by going above and beyond your goals, you could earn commission pay that far exceeds your fixed salary.

Moving into sales often means taking a reduction in the salary you are used to earning. Of course, the upside is that you might increase your overall earnings by 30 to 100 percent in a sales role. Yet, the idea of a lower base salary is a big psychological barrier to many people considering a career in sales. The fact that they have put in a number of years of hard work to get to their current salary level has become an emotional issue. It is firmly attached to their ego. Their salary is a sign of who they are. It contributes to their self-esteem.

To overcome this psychological barrier and make the transition, you must focus less on the security of a salary and more on the potential of commissions. In sales, commissions are king.

Car Allowance or Car Provided

Some companies provide a monthly car allowance to cover the average expenses of the salesperson's car. This is usually done for field sales positions where the salesperson is expected to travel a lot by car. Other companies provide the salesperson a company car. This ensures that the salesperson has a safe and attractive car to drive. A company that sells large, bulky products or pieces of equipment might provide the salesperson with a small van or other means to store and move this equipment.

Car allowances should not be considered income when you are making a decision about a sales position. It is possible that a car allowance will put you in a nicer car than you have ever had before. This is a nice perk for you and your family. However, someone in an outside sales position can easily drive 40,000 or more miles per year. This kind of mileage will quickly decrease the value of a car. Even though a car allowance might be higher than your actual payments, the balance should be set aside for service and a savings program for your next car.

Whether you are given a car allowance or a company car, you will be allowed to use the car for personal and family activities, too.

Bonuses

Bonuses are another form of incentive compensation like commissions. Most of the time, bonuses are offered in addition to commissions. Bonuses are usually paid for sales performance over a longer time period than commissions. This could be three months (a quarter), six months, or a year. Bonuses are also tied to a specific goal. For example, a cosmetics company might be introducing its first line of products for men, a line of aftershave balms and cleansers. The problem is that the sales force has never sold products for men. To succeed with this new product line, the salespeople must approach a whole new group of customers. This in turn requires a big change of behavior on the part of each salesperson. To make it worth their while to learn these new behaviors and target an entirely different line of customers, the company could offer a quarterly bonus of $X,000 for each salesperson who attains a certain level of sales of the new products. In this case, the cosmetics company might be paying a salary, commissions, and bonuses to all of its salespeople who meet their targets.

Another example of bonus compensation is an annual bonus. A company could reward all salespeople with a bonus at the end of the year if the entire company achieves its planned level of sales. Why do this? It creates positive pressure and encouragement among salespeople. No one wants to let the other salespeople down. So a sales representative who might be at only 80 percent of quota would be encouraged to continue working hard to help everyone (including himself) get the annual bonus. This bonus could be equal to a percentage of sales; more often it is a fixed amount.

Awards

Well-managed companies have awards programs. This is usually a competitive situation. The most common example is a Salesperson of the Year award to the salesperson with the highest level of sales and profitability. Often, the winner receives a plaque or trophy and a cash prize. Or she might be offered a trip for two to a resort area.

Here are some other awards that companies might give to reward and motivate their sales teams:

- Rookie of the year—best new salesperson

- Product specific—highest sales of the new widgetgizmo

- Most improved salesperson—the person with the most growth of the year. This doesn't always equate to Salesperson of the Year. But it might, and one individual could get both awards.

Other awards might be available to anyone who attains certain levels of sales. Mary Kay is famous for the pink cars it awards to its top performers. These are a highly visible (and coveted) sign of status and achievement.

Stock Awards

A stock award is actual shares of stock. Usually, a stock award is a one-time event and could be part of a performance award. The salesperson is given a number of shares, which are available immediately for the person to sell for cash or keep as an investment.

Stock Options

Publicly traded companies often offer stock options to salespeople on an annual basis. Some offer stock options as an award for attaining certain levels of sales. A stock option is not the same thing as a share of stock. It is the right to purchase a share of stock at a certain price.

The reason stock options can be particularly motivating is because they can become quite valuable. For example, if someone is given a stock option with an exercise price of $10 in 1999 and can convert it to real stock three years later at $15, there is a net gain of $5 per share. Even though the stock is worth $15, the individual has to pay only $10 for it. Stock options are usually in the hundreds or thousands of shares, so that $5 per share can easily multiply into thousands or even hundreds of thousands of dollars by the time the options are exercised—not a bad return for helping a company grow in value. Imagine the stock doubling or tripling in value. This is what happened at Microsoft.

Because of these options, the salesperson is motivated to remain loyal to the company. This helps the company reduce its turnover. Typically, stock options *vest,* or become available, over a period of four years, so you must wait before cashing them in. Usually 25 percent of the options vest each year.

Pay Ranges

Depending on the sales position and the products or services involved, full-time salespeople can earn from $24,000 to over $1,000,000 per year. Part-time salespeople representing home-sale products such as Amway, Tupperware, Longaberger Baskets, BeautiControl, Weekenders, and Mary Kay might add from several hundred dollars to tens of thousands of dollars a year to their other income.

As noted earlier in this chapter, organizations around the country conduct annual salary surveys. We've examined several of these sources to come up with the following chart of what you can expect for compensation if you enter the field of sales. Keep in mind that this is total compensation—not salary alone—and it can vary quite a bit from industry to industry, company to company, and region to region. Sales compensation is also heavily dependent on performance, and these statistics include both experienced sales professionals with established territories and newcomers to the field who will probably have lower-than-average incomes until they have brought a territory up to full production and honed their sales skills.

Job Title	Criteria	Compensation Range
Outside sales representative	Average annual compensation by size of company	$79,000 to $91,000
Outside sales representative	Average annual compensation based on performance	$57,500 (low-level performer) to $126,000 (top performer)
Key-accounts sales representative	Median annual compensation	$93,321
State sales manager	Median annual compensation	$62,000
Regional sales manager	Median annual compensation	$112,500

Let's go beyond these "average" and "median" figures to look at two examples.

Someone selling cosmetics for a premier cosmetics line such as Estée Lauder at a major department store might make $40,000 per year. As described earlier, this is an inside sales position. It is a great job, in the same location every day with customers coming to you, so there is no cold calling. The only negative is that the upper income level is somewhat limited.

At the other extreme is real estate. A very successful real-estate agent might earn more than $1 million a year by specializing in expensive luxury homes or commercial real estate. In this case, the real-estate agent does need to actively seek customers and might have to have the skills to manage a support staff. The real-estate agent also experiences much greater fluctuations in income than does the cosmetics salesperson, perhaps selling no properties for two, three, or even six months and then closing on half a dozen properties in the next 30 days. There is typically no base salary to cushion the extremes of these income peaks and valleys. And finally, the million-dollar commercial real-estate salesperson is the exception rather than the norm. Average compensation for full-time real-estate sales professionals was $60,000 in a 1999 survey by *REALTOR* magazine, but fully 30 percent of those in the business for more than 10 years earned annual compensation above $100,000.

In chapter 8 we talk about career paths—how you can move up the career ladder from your start as a sales representative. More information about compensation is discussed in that chapter.

How Does Compensation Affect Your Move into Sales?

Compensation will affect your sales career decisions several ways. To understand this, you must assess your personal situation and then gauge the sales opportunities you have access to. Finally, you must evaluate the personal fit of the various sales positions as well as the financial fit.

Are you single with a low cost of living? Or are you married with three children and a stay-at-home spouse? Obviously, a single person with few financial obligations could take a sales job with a riskier compensation program such as 100 percent commissions. Someone who is the sole breadwinner for the family will want to find a sales position that pays a decent base salary. In a two-income household, one of the two people could make a career move into sales as long as the income from the other person can cover most of the fixed household expenses.

You will more than likely assume some risk when you start your sales career. For example, an engineer at a chemical company decides to apply for a sales job in her company. Her base salary as an engineer might be $50,000. Perhaps she is a level-two engineer. If she waited a few years for another promotion or two, she might increase her income to $65,000. So she has to weigh the current opportunity against the future. Let's look at the sales position:

Base salary	$40,000
Car allowance	$ 6,000 ($500 per month)
Potential first-year commissions	$25,000 (if she achieves the quota set for her)
Total	**$71,000**

The car allowance might seem like income. But she must keep in mind that this job might run her car into the ground. So the car allowance is just what it says it is. That money should be used for car expenses and a savings program to replace the car later.

Remember that the commissions aren't guaranteed. But there might be some safety in the commission numbers. Will she be taking over a territory that already has customers and ongoing sales? If so, those ongoing sales might pay some of the commission dollars. She will need to maintain these sales and find new sales opportunities as well. And she will have to get used to the fact that the salary line on her paycheck will go down, and commissions each pay period might or might not equal the amount she was accustomed to making.

The upside with this job is the potential for overachievement. What if she works hard and exceeds her quota? Her annual commissions might add up to $30,000 or $35,000. Also, as she builds her territory and sales continue to rise, her foundation of customers will provide for higher total commissions. Now we are looking at a job that could have a tremendous positive impact on her finances. But there is no hiding the fact that it is less of a "sure thing" than the job with a steady salary.

Another example would be a person who leaves his company to take a sales job in a different industry. Let's say an office manager is considering leaving his job to go into real-estate sales. He has passed the test and has a real-estate company willing to sponsor him. If he is married and his wife is making a reasonable income relative to their household expenses, this could be a worthwhile risk. If it doesn't work, he can go back to being an office manager. Perhaps his wife's job also covers the medical benefits for the family. The only risk is the lost income during the time he is trying to get his first sale. His office-manager salary is $37,000. It might take him five months to get that first sale. Let's say the average home price in his community is $125,000. Let's also assume that he will more than likely always be splitting the 7 percent commission with another agent (more often than not there are two agents, a buyer's agent and a seller's agent, involved in every sale). So, 3.5 percent on a sale of $125,000 would bring $4,375 to the real-estate agency. The agency will take some of that money for office expenses and operating profit. They will then pay the agent perhaps 70 percent of that amount, or $3,060. What this means is that he needs to sell one house a month to equal the income of his job as an office manager. If he can persist through the first year in real estate, he could find the next several years very rewarding. This is definitely doable.

However, what if this man is a single dad with two children in elementary school? Let's say he has little in savings. The company where he works as an office manager has good health benefits for him and his children. He is considering a job in real-estate sales to gain a more flexible schedule for spending time with the children. This is a much riskier proposition. To quit his job, lose the benefits, and face several months without income doesn't make sense. It would be better to take a different strategy. He could look for a job as an office manager at a real-estate agency. At the same time, he could save his money. In a few years he would be in a much better position to try a move into real-estate sales.

Other very good opportunities for single parents or sole breadwinners would be selling credible home-based products for companies such as Tupperware, Mary Kay, Amway, Weekenders, or many others. (See the appendix, "Resources for Your Sales Job Search and Career," for information on some home-sales companies.) While keeping the security and benefits of a full-time job, the salesperson has the potential to add several hundred dollars of income a month while building strong sales skills. To be successful in this kind of sales, it's important to fit the product and company to your personality and skill sets.

Don't enter a sales job with too much financial stress interfering with the way you think. A small amount of stress, however, is good. It is a motivator. A common joke among sales managers is that they want their salespeople to buy more expensive homes so that they have higher mortgage payments. The idea is that their salespeople will be hungrier for sales to help pay for the bigger house. But when you are starting out in sales, a lot of financial stress is a distraction that will make it difficult for you to learn your new job. You could become desperate. Customers will sense this emotion and it will drive them away.

Finally, don't get pulled into "get-rich-quick" schemes. There are a lot of them advertised every day. Just because the "opportunity" is listed in *USA Today* or your local newspaper doesn't mean it is credible. Many of these schemes require you to make an investment—sometimes thousands of dollars. These companies are more interested in getting your money than they are in your success.

Wrap-up and To Do

You have learned that there are a lot of components to sales compensation. Although you can see the potential upside of a sales job, you also realize that there is an element of financial risk. Now, as you move forward in your research on a career in sales, you should do the following:

1. If you are married, discuss this career move with your spouse. You will want all the support and patience he or she can give you.

2. Look carefully at your budget. Make sure you understand what income you actually need from month to month. Many people are surprised at the wasted money in their budget. They can actually live on less than they realize.

3. Look at your savings. Be sure you have savings to fall back on if you find that your monthly cash flow becomes negative once in a while.

4. Contact the friends you have in sales and ask them what the transition was like. Get their advice.

5. If you think there is the possibility of getting a sales job in the company you work for, take one or two of the salespeople to lunch. Get their thoughts on sales compensation in your industry. If you know them well enough, they might share some of their compensation information with you. If they share their compensation details with you, be sure to keep this confidential.

6. If you are considering a home-based sales opportunity that you intend to work at part-time, talk to several people who are already doing this. Get realistic information on the following:

    a. How many hours they invest in the work every week.

    b. How long it took for them to start making some money.

    c. How much money you can realistically make after three to six months of effort.

CHAPTER 5 The Art and Science of Sales: Understanding and Assessing Your Fit for the Field

One of the greatest myths in sales is that you must be a good-looking, smooth-talking, charming person to be successful. That is simply not true. Unfortunately, this myth has been promoted in movies, books, and television shows. Of course, it never hurts to have these characteristics. They can be quite valuable. But alone, they can be very limiting and in many cases result in failure. A person who uses only these traits and skills is relying completely on the *art* of selling. In today's world of commerce, mastering the *science* of sales is critical to success.

It is very important to understand the balance between these two components—art and science—as well as the fundamental traits and skills that indicate a good chance of success in the field. In this chapter we review these traits (ingrained tendencies) and skills (learned abilities) as they apply to both the art and the science of selling.

At the end of the chapter, we've provided a checklist against which you can compare yourself. Remember, you don't have to score a 10 on every item. Also, some skills can be learned and others can be perfected. In fact, new salespeople can boost their chances of success by applying themselves to learning the science of sales as they develop the art.

The Art of Sales

Perhaps you have a friend who could "sell ice to an Eskimo." Or maybe you know someone who is able to smoothly and easily talk people into doing things for them or doing things their way. These people are clearly demonstrating the art of sales.

Artful Personality Traits

Personality traits—ingrained characteristics—that are important in the art of sales include the following:

- Integrity
- Persistence
- Interest in people
- Ambition
- Desire to win
- Desire to succeed—immediately
- Enthusiasm
- Moxie
- Charisma
- Persuasiveness

The following sections examine each of these in more detail.

Integrity

If there is a trait where the score of 10 is important, it is integrity. This is especially true regarding relationships with customers and teammates in the company. Customers can sense integrity in the way a salesperson manages business dealings. Integrity earns respect and support from colleagues. Over the long haul, honest salespeople beat dishonest ones every time.

Persistence

Persistence is a natural willingness and desire to keep after a goal. In the case of sales, the goal is customer contact. You must be willing to call again and again, by phone and in person. Guess what? Many customers respect professional persistence. They want to do business with a winner. Ted's story is a great example:

> *One of the best sales reps I ever hired was initially in third place when the interview process started. By the end of the process, he was a close second to the lead candidate for the job. Then I checked references. The woman on the other end of the phone said, 'If you had asked me two years ago if I would ever give a reference to a fellow from that company, I would have laughed in your face. We hated his company. But he kept coming back to the office. He solved all the problems his predecessors had caused. And he kept coming back. Finally, one day I had to go out and meet this nut who persisted and was not getting any business for his effort. Today, we buy almost all our products from him. He is the best!' And, after that reference, I hired him.*

Interest in People

Sales is a people business. You must like people and be able to get along with them. Better yet, people should intrigue you, and you should have the attitude that most people are basically good.

Ambition

Ambition is a critical trait for salespeople. It is a bit different than a "desire to win" (which is described next). Ambition is related to long-term goals or a series of wins that lead to a long-term goal. An ambitious salesperson sets a goal of making a defined number of sales for the month or year that will lead to a certain income and recognition. Ambition also can be associated with lifestyle goals that will be achieved if a higher sales-driven income is attained. For example, the salesperson's ambitions might be a larger house and a nicer car. Other goals could be early retirement or better colleges for the children.

Desire to Win

This is another critical trait, and it starts with a competitive spirit, which could have been developed in youth by playing sports. It could also be developed by the influence of a healthy competitiveness among family members in school or games. People with a desire to win will invest the time to get the job done. They also like the victory and the achievement of winning. In fact, one of the things that motivates them is imagining the victory. The desire to win is immediate and related to the selling opportunity at hand or a short-term sales contest. If you have a healthy desire to win, you can be taught how to ask a customer to make a purchase decision. This is called *closing*.

Desire to Succeed—Immediately

The key word here is "immediately." We all know people like this, whether or not they have the other traits we are discussing. The desire to succeed is different from the general desire to win. These people need the instant gratification of winning immediately. That means right now! And they can drive you crazy. At the same time, they will insist on getting an answer. In a selling situation, they won't be satisfied with any answer but "yes."

If this trait is exaggerated into a "win at all costs" mentality, meeting the needs of the customer becomes secondary to the sale. Customers can sense this attitude, and after a while it turns them off. A healthy desire to win is absolutely necessary to get ahead in sales. This is an important sales driver. But the desire for immediate success, every minute, can be alienating if not used properly.

Enthusiasm

Enthusiasm is reflected in the ease with which you get excited about life, your friends, family, work, projects, and so forth. You would see a problem or challenge as an opportunity. Enthusiastic people tend to go several steps further in serving their customers. Also, this trait is infectious. People and customers like being around an enthusiastic person.

Moxie

Moxie is a kind of daring mixed with energy or spunk. People with moxie will push the envelope. This story of one of Ted's experiences is a good example of moxie in action:

> *I recall a time when I was acting as a sales specialist and working with a local sales rep for a surgical instrument company. My company's products were just a few of the hundreds of products that she was responsible for. We were meeting with a neurosurgeon to try to sell him on trying one of the shunts from my company. I was doing most of the presenting. I felt that I had reached the surgeon's pressure limit for the day and was beginning to back off. I didn't think we could push him any further for a decision. As I began to sit back, Robbie jumped right in and kept going with a smile on her face. She got the sale! She demonstrated moxie.*

Charisma

Individuals with charisma seem to be able to inspire and charm others to follow them with enthusiasm. People with charisma almost hypnotize others into being followers. This is a great personality characteristic for a leader to have. However, as history has shown us time and again, charismatic leadership has had both very good and very bad consequences. So you need to be able to back up your charisma with some integrity.

Persuasiveness

Finally, we should throw the skill of persuasiveness into the mix. People who are strong in the art of selling are naturally persuasive. They learned this skill early and have practiced it since they were babies. Perhaps they were in a large family where persuasiveness was an important means to getting the attention and support they needed. Maybe they had parents who challenged them constructively all the time. These people seem to be able to persuade with a smile and some drama. They are also extremely quick on their feet. They can turn a forceful objection into a point in their favor in a split second.

Attractiveness

Let's add to these characteristics one more trait that is somewhat controversial. People who are "naturals" at the art of sales also very typically have the physical trait of being attractive, whether it is drop-dead good looks or a natural smile. Or it could be that they are physically imposing. In a man's case, he could be tall and muscular or just very large overall.

Strengthening Your "Art" Skills

As you have read this, you have probably thought of some people you know who would be good sales artists. Perhaps you recognize some of the traits in yourself. This list of traits shows that the "art of sales" formula is a combination of personality characteristics and physical characteristics. You might think that it's not possible to increase your "artistry" because it relies on inherent characteristics. But in fact you can work to improve many of these traits—such as persuasiveness, enthusiasm, persistence, and interest in people. And you'll find that strengthening your "art" skills along with your "science" skills will make you a better and more well-rounded sales professional.

As mentioned in the introduction to this chapter, artistry in sales is not enough to be a sales professional in today's competitive marketplace across all industries. Artistry in sales might get someone off to a fast start in a new sales position. But if that person doesn't have the balance of the science of selling, they will ultimately fail. What happens is that these people lean too heavily on a natural set of traits and never develop other traits and skills necessary to succeed over the long term. This is a kind of laziness. On a resume it might show up as someone jumping from job to job too often. The salesperson might have won an award for best sales for certain months or quarters (three-month periods) but might not have made quota for the year. After starting the race with a lot of flash, fanfare, and success, this individual goes out with a mediocre finish. You might have heard someone like this described as a "flash in the pan."

So how do you create a long-lasting and successful sales career? The answer lies in the science of selling.

The Science of Sales

Yes, there is a science to selling. In fact, there is a science to just about anything. Science is defined as a "branch of knowledge conducted on objective principles involving systemized observation of and experiment with phenomena." Sales can be treated as a science. In fact, the most successful businesses in any industry do just that. They give their salespeople very good direction and excellent selling tools to use with customers. In the *Sales Manager's Problem Solver,* publisher Gerhard Gschwandtner says, "There is no such thing as the 'Natural Born Salesperson,' like there is no 'natural born surgeon.' Research has proven that good selling skills are the result of ongoing learning, professional coaching, and continuous practice." He is talking about implementing what we call the science of sales.

To keep this from sounding too scary, let us assure you, even companies with what might seem to be the simplest products approach selling as a science. Skin-care products and cosmetics don't seem too complicated, do they? Perhaps they aren't. But Avon, Mary Kay, Clinique, Estée Lauder, and others have turned selling these products into a science. These companies have done careful research to understand their customers' needs. Then they formulated products to meet these needs. They worked hard with their sales forces to understand the right process for selling, and they created the training programs and support systems for their salespeople. If you work for these companies and carefully follow their direction, you will succeed. The same goes for Ethicon (a division of Johnson & Johnson), Ford Motors, Wilson Sporting Goods, Novartis pharmaceuticals, Kodak industrial films, Delta Faucet, Tupperware, and on and on.

And that is the point. You don't have to develop the science. You have to learn it. And employers are very willing to teach you.

That leads us to what you add to the science equation. You have to take full advantage of a number of other personality characteristics, physical traits, and skills.

Traits That Will Help You Learn the Science of Sales

Certain personality *traits* will better equip you to learn the art of sales. To succeed, you must be

- Disciplined
- A good listener
- Methodical
- Proactive
- Self-starting
- Reliable
- Intelligent
- Forgiving
- Self-knowing

The following sections discuss the personality traits that are directly related to the science of sales.

Disciplined

Disciplined individuals demonstrate a lot of self-control. They can pursue the tasks necessary to achieve a goal even though the tasks might be very difficult. Losing weight takes discipline. In this case, it is the discipline to change eating and exercise habits and replace them with a different set of habits. People who stick to an exercise regimen display discipline. Also, pursuing the mental exercise of listening to educational tapes or regularly reading self-improvement books shows discipline. In sales, discipline is shown by the willingness to pick up the phone and make a set number of calls every day to people you don't know very well to ask for an appointment.

A Good Listener

Good listeners are truly interested in what the other person has to say and can also read between the lines for hidden messages. A person who says "I'm not hungry" might really mean that the food in front of him isn't desirable. When customers say they aren't interested in a product, they might be saying that they don't truly understand how the product will benefit them. To listen well means that you can't be constantly thinking about what you want to say next. It also means watching body language. Customers who lean toward you while they talk are genuinely interested in the interaction they are having with you. Part of listening is a trait; but listening can be improved almost as if it were a skill.

Methodical

People who are *methodical* like to follow a process. They understand that there is one best path or one proven method to get from point "A" to point "B." Sometimes it's tempting to skip the steps in a process, especially those we don't find interesting or aren't really convinced are worthwhile. Methodical people stay with the process even when they can't see the immediate rewards. This is an important trait in selling, where you have to do a lot of groundwork and legwork before you even get the opportunity to present your product or service to a client.

Proactive

Someone who is *proactive* will see an opportunity or challenge in advance and do something about it now. For example, salesperson A determines in a sales call with a customer that the competitive rep B is offering a price discount to take A's customers away. Rep A can react to each situation as it comes up. Or, better yet, she can be proactive and do two things. First, she can protect her business by calling all her customers to remind them of the reasons they do business with her. Second, she can call rep B's customers and tell them that she has heard of the new pricing. Why would she do the second? Frequently the competition doesn't offer the same discounts to existing customers as it does to potential new customers. B's customers will now call him asking about the discount. Suddenly, he will be busy dealing with his own disgruntled customers instead of calling on A's customers. These steps are both proactive and competitive.

Self-Starting

Being *self-starting* means getting to work without someone telling you to do it. We all seem to be self-starting when it involves a hobby, a game of golf, or getting to garage sales early. It is amazing how early people can get up on a Saturday morning to do something they think is fun. In sales, you don't always have a manager looking over your shoulder. In fact, sales organizations can't afford close management like this. Instead, they need people who like to get up and get out to their customers. In an inside sales job, being self-starting means getting out on the showroom floor and mingling with customers. Or it could mean picking up the phone and making calls to prospective customers.

Reliable

Customers need to buy from reliable people and reliable companies. If they have questions about a product or service, they need to get the answers as soon as possible. Also, salespeople must keep their promises of providing information or service. We are always amazed at how many salespeople drop the ball on a customer. The salesperson thinks the customer will forget the promise. She assures the customer that she will look into the issue. Then she fails to follow up. Customers remember this. They also remember the people they *can* rely on. It adds value to the relationship, just as it does to a friendship. You are always frustrated with friends who aren't reliable. You love planning things with those who are.

Intelligent

When referring to intelligence, we don't mean that you must have been a straight-A student in high school or college to be successful in sales. What you must be able to do is intelligently assess your customers' needs and recommend the right products or services to solve their problems. "One-size-fits-all" selling is not intelligent; it doesn't take into account the very different needs and circumstances of each customer. As an intelligent salesperson, you must know where you can get support and assistance from within your company. You must also understand your company's sales strategy and the kinds of customers you'll be targeting.

Forgiving

In selling situations, it is possible to run into some very rude people. Someone who was nice to you one day might be unpleasant the next time you call. Some people are just negative toward salespeople. This attitude is often prompted by the fear that they are going to be pressured into something, and their natural reaction is immediately to be defensive. There are other reasons for customers' rudeness and bad attitude. They might just be having a bad day. Perhaps they had an argument with their spouse the night before. Maybe a loved one is very ill. Or their boss might have been critical of them. When customers are in a bad mood, they frequently take out their frustration on the nearest salesperson. You must be able to forgive this for two reasons. First, there is nothing you can do about someone's attitude except be pleasant, regardless of the situation. Second, it is good for the salesperson's own mental attitude to be forgiving instead of angry or too disappointed. A forgiving attitude goes a long way toward helping you handle the rejection you might feel in a sales job.

Self-Knowing

When entering a new career such as sales, you must be honest with yourself about your current capabilities. Then you must be realistic in your aspirations. This will keep you grounded. But don't discount yourself. If you have the capability to learn quickly and are easily coached, you can take a healthy ambition and desire to win and turn these traits into a successful selling situation. This self-knowledge will be critical as you map out your strategy to get into a sales job.

Skills That Are Important to the Science of Sales

Skills—learnable abilities—that are important in the science of sales include the following:

- Organization

- Questioning

- Presentation

- Communication

- Problem-solving

- Sales process

- Product knowledge

- Market knowledge

- Company knowledge

- Follow-up

The following sections discuss each of these skills in detail.

Organization

Salespeople are very independent. Most sales jobs allow a fair amount of freedom from direct management. With that freedom comes the responsibility of being organized. This is especially true for field sales positions.

In sales, you must be able to plan your weeks and days to be productive. Then you need to be able to stick with the plan you have created. In your office or car, you must have all the product literature, manuals, and samples organized for easy retrieval. Finally, you must appear to be organized. When you open a briefcase and the customer sees that everything is neat, well ordered, and easily retrievable, you make a positive impression about your abilities as a sales professional.

Questioning

There are several points in the sales process where it is important to have good questioning skills. The first questions you must ask help you decide whether a prospect is qualified to be a customer. The second group of questions you'll ask helps you better understand a prospect's needs. The third group of questions helps you make sure that the customer understands what you are presenting. Knowing how to ask the right questions at the right time is a great skill and one of the best you can learn.

Presentation

How you present a product or service to customers will make a big difference in whether they understand how they will benefit from it. Whether you are selling a plastic food-storage container or a $400,000 surgical laser, you have to be able to present the product and its benefits effectively.

Communication

You should bring to the sales job good writing, speaking, and Internet communication skills. Selling is a job of communicating with customers, teammates, and superiors. This communication is verbal in the form of presentations and general sharing of information. It is also written, in follow-up letters, proposals, reports, memos, and e-mail. Good salespeople must be able to express themselves clearly using all forms of communication. That includes good spelling and grammar. It also includes being able to articulate an idea or thought quickly and clearly. For many sales jobs, it means being able to make a complex service or technical product understandable to customers at all levels.

Problem-Solving

In sales roles that involve selling a lot of products on a regular basis to a customer, problem-solving is critical. When the volume of products is high, there is an equally high probability that something can go wrong. The salesperson leads the effort to find out what is wrong and to straighten it out. Problems can also come up in the middle of delivering a service, such as audiovisual services to a hotel or convention. Again, the salesperson will be in the middle of finding a solution to keep the customer happy. Customers appreciate problem-solvers. In fact, when you take a new sales position, it is better to get a territory with a lot of problems than to take over a territory that had a super salesperson. Why? In the territory with problems, you can be a problem-solver and gain the customers' trust. Your sales have only one way to go, and that is up.

Sales Process

This is a skill that you can improve upon constantly. Most companies have carefully thought-out sales processes for their sales force to follow. There is a process for every product. It is up to each individual salesperson to marry the process to his or her personal style. This process can be learned, practiced, and improved upon.

Product Knowledge

A good company does a thorough job of teaching a sales trainee all the features and benefits of its products. You must have the aptitude to learn this information. You will have to memorize some of it. If there is a lot of detail, you will need to know immediately where to find answers in manuals and other product literature. Over time, you will find that you have memorized much of the critical information. Learning about products and services is fun and rewarding, and your knowledge will boost your confidence in each sales call you make.

Market Knowledge

Depending on how you enter a sales position, you might or might not have market knowledge. If you are a woman considering selling cosmetics for BeautiControl, you probably have a basic understanding about the market. This is because you are already an active consumer of the products and you probably discuss cosmetics with your friends. This is great! Ted's experience was quite different. "When I started my first job, I had no clue about the market for the surgical implants I was going to sell. I had to learn this skill from the company and on my own. I didn't know such implants existed."

Let's go back to the BeautiControl example. Even if you know about the market in general, you'll build your sales skills by learning more. You will be astonished at the interesting things you will learn and how valuable that information will be in planning and carrying out your sales strategies.

Company Knowledge

Training programs for most companies include information about the history of the company, its facilities, and its track record of success over the years. Training typically involves meeting individuals from a variety of departments. All of this helps new salespeople feel like they are part of a team. It also helps them learn where to go to get support within the company.

Follow-up

Earlier in the chapter we discussed the trait of reliability. Follow-up skills are a key part of demonstrating reliability and are a great way to stand out from the crowd of "average" salespeople. Nowhere is this more true than with direct-selling organizations such as Longaberger baskets, Weekenders, BeautiControl, and Avon cosmetics. Most of the time, these companies' products can be bought only through an independent representative for the company—the customer is a "captive" to the company's method of selling. Yet if the salesperson has poor follow-up skills, the customer becomes discouraged and might quit buying from the company altogether.

Louise remembers two experiences that show the dramatic difference follow-up can make. Once, trying to buy a Longaberger basket because she was so impressed with one she had received as a gift, she contacted the rep in her area by phone and by e-mail and never received a callback. Naturally, that meant she bought no products, and that rep lost what could have been a very good customer. On another occasion, Louise's daughter attended a Creative Memories party in another city and then wanted to buy scrapbook products when she returned home. One phone call and the Creative Memories rep responded with a catalog and regular follow-up that resulted in many orders and hundreds of dollars in business.

To help with follow-up and reliability, many companies provide specialized calendars, to-do lists, computer software, and other tools that help their sales reps keep track of customers and projects. They do a great job of teaching the skill of good follow-up.

Other Important Traits and Skills

Some traits and skills don't fit neatly into the "art" or "science" of selling but are nonetheless extremely important for success in sales. These include

- Self-confidence
- A positive outlook
- Caring
- Good judgment
- Work ethic

The following sections look at these traits and skills in more detail.

Self-Confidence

The trait of self-confidence is very important in sales. Sales can have a lot of ups and downs. Sports teams that get behind in a game but display self-confidence can frequently come back to win. The same goes for salespeople. Self-confident people believe that if they keep doing the right things, success will come their way. They are also sure enough of themselves that they can admit to mistakes and seek constructive advice when needed. Self-confidence is a reflection of healthy self-esteem.

A Positive Outlook

People with a positive outlook or positive thinking purposely organize their lives around positive influences. These can be social and business groups. Or they can be positive books and tapes. At the extreme, someone with a really positive outlook on life and work could be criticized as being a bit "rah-rah." We will take that person on our sales team anytime! And they are usually successful.

Caring

There has to be room to care for the customer. Some customers will be difficult to care about. However, customers can sense if you care. They like it. The following story demonstrates a combination of good listening and caring.

> *A sales rep was calling on a Jewish doctor who was quite friendly but had never purchased a product from her. He lived in an inland city in California. He complained to her that he never could find good Jewish bread in his city. The next time she returned to his office, she brought a loaf of Jewish bread from one of the best Jewish bakeries in Los Angeles. Soon after, he started buying from her. He became a very loyal account.*

Good Judgment

Good judgment is usually a combination of an inherent trait and a learned skill. Some people instinctively seem to use good judgment and make wise decisions that minimize negative outcomes. Others always seem to get themselves in even deeper trouble by an unwise comment, poorly thought-out response, or purely reflexive action. If you're one of the former, congratulations! You can work to sharpen your judgment by thinking about why you make the choices you do. If you're not an instinctively good decision-maker, you can build this ability by analyzing the responses of those with good judgment and taking the time to think about all the consequences before you act.

Work Ethic

Some people are naturally hard workers. They apply themselves diligently to any task or project they take on. Many others get "charged up" only when the task interests them, and they will work extremely hard on projects they feel are important. Still others are not that interested in working hard. They get by with a minimum of effort in everything they do.

How do you measure up? A lot of your attitude toward work has to do with how you were brought up and the values of your parents and other role models. A strong work ethic is hard to teach, but anyone can work to improve the energy and attention they give to each task.

Putting It All Together

Let's look at how all these traits and skills, the art and science of sales, come together to make an effective salesperson.

Discipline, Proactivity, and Organization

As a professional salesperson, you must have the discipline to carefully study the sales process and understand how the product's features and benefits fit into that process. Then you must be methodical about using that selling system day in and day out. You must know your company so that you know where to get support and assistance. You must listen carefully during the training programs when you are taught about the kind of customers you will be targeting. These are the customers who are most likely to buy your products. Then you must be able to communicate with your customers and your teammates. This is the science of sales.

Further, to be a good salesperson, you must be proactive and organized enough to plan a productive week. You have to be ready to reach out to prospective customers to make appointments. You must have the discipline to get up every day and implement the sales process. For the inside salesperson, this means getting to work early and being prepared to work with customers the minute the door opens, as well as picking up the phone and calling recent customers to be sure they are happy with their purchases. For the field salesperson, this means getting out of the house or office and in front of customers. This is what we meant earlier when we invoked the old saying that "half of sales is showing up." This also is the science of sales.

Keeping Promises

One of the biggest complaints that customers have is that a salesperson did not keep a promise to do something. Perhaps the customer asked for some additional data related to a product. A customer might ask for the name of another customer to call as a reference. Sometimes, to get the sale, salespeople promise additional features or accessories. Then they fail to put these on the purchase order and the customer doesn't get what he was promised. *Keeping promises is critical.* It relates to the salesperson's integrity and reliability.

As a sales manager, Ted frequently worked with his sales reps in the field. Occasionally he would hear them promise a doctor some additional information… but he would not see them make a note in their personal organizer to do what they had just promised. He would make a note himself. Then, at the end of the week, he would ask the sales reps whether they had followed through on the promise to the doctor. Most often, they would say, "No, I let it slip through the cracks." If it's not written down, chances are it will be forgotten.

Customers and prospective customers remember promises that have been kept. They consider this part of the partnership they have developed with their salesperson. Their sales rep becomes a "go-to" person for answers and solutions to problems. Really professional reps will help their customers with problems that have nothing to do with their products or services.

Customers also have a deep memory for promises that aren't kept. People who rely completely on the art of the sale are so involved in the immediacy of selling that they frequently don't care about keeping promises. They might get a sale the first time and possibly the second. But when they go for the third order and there have been a couple of broken promises along the way, the customer will say "No." The salesperson has lost credibility.

Showing Appreciation and Attention to Detail

Another piece of sales science is good follow-up with customers. How many purchases have you made in your life? How often have you received a personalized thank-you note from the salesperson you dealt with? (Computer-generated thank-you notes don't count.) We imagine you have received very few. When you did receive one, you were impressed. We know we are. Here is a story from Ted's experience.

> *Once I suggested a friend of mine send a thank-you note to a customer. My friend was in charge of national accounts for a large medical company. Her job was to build relationships with the large hospital chains and purchasing groups. She had never been in sales. You could almost say she was a reluctant salesperson. She had absolutely no art. But she had a lot of science. She took my advice, and a funny thing happened. The day the note landed on the desk of the purchasing executive, my friend's bosses arrived in his office for a visit. Her bosses were the VP and President of the company. The purchasing executive opened the card right in front of them. Then he told the VP and the President that this card was a good example of why she was the key to their success with his purchasing group. In so many words he said, "She is why we buy from you."*
>
> *A simple, sincere card. Perfect science.*

A lot of what you have just read could be captured in the concept of attention to detail. When you know your product inside and out, when you know the competitor's products better than they do, when you know your customers better than anyone, when you do what you say you are going to do, and when everything you do is complete, you are showing attention to detail.

Harvey McKay is a legendary sales leader whose books frequently spell out the science of sales. Harvey defined 66 things that the salespeople who worked for him needed to know about every customer. And he carefully explained how to gather those 66 pieces of information over time. His famous McKay 66 will always work—now and 100 years from now. One of the things Harvey drills into audiences is that the salesman or woman who knows the customer best will eventually get the business. This is attention to detail in action. It works, and it is an important part of the science of sales.

Discipline, Determination, and a Healthy Desire to Win

The key to the science of sales is to have the discipline to follow the methodology. While reading this section, you might have been thinking that this makes a lot of sense. Why doesn't everybody do it? Like all sciences, applying theory to reality is not easy. It takes discipline. If you have the characteristics we discussed in this chapter and can put them together in a way that takes advantage of the science of sales, you have a very good chance at succeeding in this career.

But all of the methodology in the world isn't going to help someone in a sales career if that person isn't personable, a good communicator, and willing to ask for a sale. You have to have the determination to ask a customer to buy something from you and your company. You have to be willing to take "no" for an answer at least temporarily. If "no" is the answer, you have to find out why, try to overcome the objection, and then ask for the sale again. This is where the art and science of selling come together.

Having a healthy competitive nature and a desire to win is important in sales. This is also part of the art of sales. This is not the same as the destructive behavior we described earlier as winning at all costs. Once a salesperson has done all the hard work of getting in front of a customer and presenting a product in a knowledgeable and convincing manner, it is time to ask the customer to make a decision. Will they buy the product? A good, competitive sales rep might ask the customer to buy a product three different ways in the same sales call. This is normal and good sales art.

If the scientific part of the sale was done correctly and delivered with reasonable art, more often than not the customer will say yes. Ted clearly recalls one of his first big sales victories: "I will never forget how nervous I was when I first asked a customer to make a buying decision. When she said yes, I was ecstatic! It was a big day."

The Importance of Good Leadership, Coaching, and Management

One of the most important elements of putting together these two components of selling is good management, coaching, leadership, and mentoring. Most very successful people in any endeavor have someone behind them providing advice, direction, ideas, or a kick in the rear. Sure, Wayne Gretzky was a naturally talented hockey player who became one of the greatest of all time. But he would have never become the greatest without dedicated coaches, hard-working teammates, and a supportive family. He would be the first to tell you that. One missed step in his career, one bad coach, and we might never have heard of Wayne Gretzky.

Even great salespeople have sales slumps. They become unbalanced in combining the art and science parts of their job. Who gets them back on track? Often it is the sales manager who can determine what's wrong and help the salesperson refocus, rebalance, and recommit.

Good management is extremely important to the success of the person who is new to sales as a career. A good manager really enjoys working constructively with his or her team members, challenging them, and watching them grow. As a manager, there is no greater honor than to see one of your salespeople get an award for achieving or exceeding sales goals. When you are interviewing for a sales position, you will most likely be interviewing with the person who would manage you. At some point in the interview, you should ask them about their management style. You should also ask them whether many people in their region have won awards. The way that question is answered will tell you a lot about your prospective manager.

Where Do You Learn the Art and the Science?

Most great scientists and artists went to school somewhere to get a good foundation of knowledge upon which to build their ideas. If you are breaking into sales for the first time, it is important for you to go where someone will give you a foundation in selling and the science behind it. Successful large companies usually have good sales organizations that invest a lot of time and money in training. Some forward-thinking medium-sized companies and small companies have seasoned sales executives who can guide a new salesperson in the science. However, most often, the smaller companies don't have the time and money to invest in training. They are too busy trying to grow from small to medium or from medium to large. What they do is recruit seasoned salespeople from the large companies. The large company is the training ground. Keep this in mind as you read this book. If you aren't that familiar with sales, where will you learn? Who will support you?

Every industry has companies that are the cornerstones of professionalism in sales. In pharmaceuticals it is Merck. In medical products and medical devices it is Johnson & Johnson. In real estate it's Coldwell Banker and Century 21. In furniture it is Ethan Allen. In cosmetics sold in the home, it is Mary Kay and BeautiControl. In department stores it is Nordstrom. In computers it is Dell and IBM. In life insurance it is Northwestern Mutual Life, New England Financial Network, New York Life, and Massachusetts Mutual Life. These and many other leading companies have long traditions of helping their salespeople become professionals. You might be surprised to see the mention of companies such as Mary Kay. However, May Kay is a top-notch company dedicated to great products and a great training and mentoring program to support its salespeople.

Ted's Story

My first two sales jobs are a good example of companies that invest in sales training and those that don't. My first job was working for a small division of big American Hospital Supply Corporation (later acquired by Baxter). There was no sales training at this division. None. It was all product training. Why? Because they typically hired seasoned sales reps who had been trained at other companies. I was one of the rare reps hired right out of graduate school. They weren't prepared to provide me with sales training. They did provide good product training, so I could discuss the products intelligently with doctors, nurses, and hospital personnel. However, they expected the new salespeople to take this product knowledge and plug it into a sales system that they had acquired somewhere else.

My second job was where I really learned the art and science of selling. It was with Northwestern Mutual Life. They believed in investing in training in both the art and the science of sales. It was not unusual for NML agents to come from a variety of walks of life. The company was willing to help you start from scratch. Like many great companies, NML knew the formula for sales success intimately. They knew that if you made enough phone calls in one day to have actual contacts with 10 prospective customers, you would end up with three appointments. They also knew that three scheduled appointments would result in one actual appointment. The other two would be cancelled or postponed. Finally, it took three actual appointments to make one sale of an insurance product. So, if you work backwards, you can figure out that to make one sale you would start out with 30 actual phone contacts. If you need to sell one life insurance or investment product a week to be successful, you'd better be willing to make enough calls to generate 30 actual phone contacts. Is that 40 calls? Or 50? Or 60? Knowing this information is one critical part of the science of selling insurance. As an agent, you knew what you had to do week in and week out. They even gave you specially designed calendars that were made to help you keep track of your work.

Then NML offered great sales training using Wilson Learning Company's Counselor Sales courses. In these courses, agents would learn the critical elements of the sales process. Finally, NML provided weekly meetings with your peers and manager to discuss sales and generate motivation. Fact was, if you hit the work numbers and applied the other elements of sales to your efforts, you would be successful. Almost sounds easy. But as mentioned earlier in the chapter, it takes discipline and forgiveness to pick up the phone knowing that a lot of people are going to say "No!"

In every industry there are several companies like Northwestern Mutual Life. You need to find one as a foundation for your career. Or, if you're joining a smaller company, you need to be sure your manager will give you the coaching and motivation you are going to need. Finally, you might need to go out on your own to find the training. This is possible with companies such as Dale Carnegie, Wilson Learning, and other respected sources (see the appendix for details). These companies offer courses to the public in many cities, and many also offer online training, newsletters, and continuous information to build your knowledge of the art and science of selling.

Career and Personality Assessments

Career-assessment instruments can help you evaluate your strengths, weaknesses, and career interests. These are administered by career professionals as well as the career guidance centers of many community colleges and universities. (You might not have to be a student to take advantage of these services.) After you complete the assessment questionnaires, you will need to review the results with a qualified counselor who has the knowledge and experience to interpret the findings accurately.

One of the most respected assessments is the Myers-Briggs Type Indicator (MBTI). This instrument evaluates your behavioral preferences to place you within one of 16 behavioral types. Knowing and understanding your Myers-Briggs type can help you in several ways as you consider a sales career and then when you are actually holding a sales position.

First of all, it's important to recognize that there is no one "perfect" type that guarantees success in sales. For instance, one of the Myers-Briggs scales measures Thinking versus Feeling preferences. This relates to how you make decisions. If you are a strong "T," you make decisions using logical, objective analysis, whereas if you fall high on the "F" scale, you are more likely to decide based on feelings rather than logic.

Think about how this might relate to sales. If you have a strong Thinking preference, you're probably naturally skilled in analyzing needs and fitting products or services to those needs. That's important in sales! But if you've neglected the opposite end of the scale and haven't tuned in to your customers' feelings, you will have a hard time building rapport and relationships that are so critical in most sales positions. Clearly, a balance of the two is ideal. If you're aware of this, you can work to develop your "weaker" side of the scale to create a more well-rounded approach that will benefit you and your customers.

Another way to use MBTI information to your advantage is to improve the way you communicate with your customers and colleagues according to their behavioral preferences. If you are working with a high "T" customer, for instance, you'll be more persuasive if you use facts and logic to sell your product or service. With a high "F" customer, you can stress less-concrete benefits and appeal to emotional needs. If you take the time to learn about the MBTI preferences, you can make very educated guesses about your customers' styles that will give you an edge in sales.

Clearly, this discussion has touched just the tip of the iceberg with regard to MBTI! If you are interested in learning more, we suggest you read up on the subject and consult with a career counselor who is certified to interpret MBTI assessments. Books and other resources are listed in the appendix.

Recognizing Your Balance

As you read this book and do other research in pursuing a sales career, you need to start to determine where you are in the balance of art and science. This is important self-knowledge. When you know where your strengths and weaknesses lie, you know where you need to invest time to improve your overall skills and the balance of your skills.

Of course you can always talk to people who know you well. However, if they aren't personally experienced with sales, they might not be able to give you good advice. In fact, if they have a bad attitude about sales borne of some myth, they might discourage you. Just because they can't handle the idea of a career in sales doesn't mean you shouldn't give it serious consideration.

Wrap-up and To Do

In this chapter you have learned that there is an important balance between the art of selling and the science of selling. Either alone is not sufficient for success. However, the science of selling is the more important of the two. Because you don't yet know this science, you need to find a place to learn it. If you are fortunate enough to have some of the characteristics and skills related to the art, you need to find a company and a manager who can help give you the right direction. The good news is that selling can be learned, and there are companies willing to provide the right people the foundation they need to be successful.

Self-Assessment Checklist

How do you stack up? Score yourself from 1–10 on each of the traits and abilities discussed in this chapter. Then check your balance of "art" and "science," inherent and learnable abilities. You'll get a good picture of how balanced you are in all of the important characteristics that make up a successful salesperson. And you'll see where you can increase your scores by working diligently to learn, from the first day of your sales career to the last.

Self-Assessment Checklist

	Inherent Traits: Art of Sales	Inherent Traits: Science of Sales	Learnable Skills	General Characteristics
Integrity				
Persistence				
Interest in people				
Ambition				
Desire to win				
Desire to succeed				
Enthusiasm				
Moxie				
Charisma				
Persuasiveness				
Disciplined				
Good listener				
Methodical				
Proactive				
Self-starting				
Reliable				
Intelligent				
Forgiving				
Self-knowing				
Organization				
Questioning				
Presentation				
Communication				
Problem-solving				
Sales process				
Product knowledge				
Market knowledge				
Company knowledge				
Consistent follow-up				
Self-confidence				
Positive outlook				
Caring				
Good judgment				
Work ethic				
TOTALS				
	Inherent Traits: Art of Sales (range: 0–100)	Inherent Traits: Science of Sales (range: 0–90)	Learnable Skills (range: 0–100)	General Characteristics (range: 0–50)

CHAPTER 6 Why Women Rule in Sales

Women are becoming a greater part of sales organizations in all industries. In this chapter we explore some possible reasons for this phenomenon and share with you the experiences of nine women who are very successful in sales in diverse industries. If you're a woman considering a career in sales, we think you'll be inspired by their success stories and be motivated to write your own!

Ted's Viewpoint

In one of my previous management positions, half of my sales force was female. It didn't start that way, but over time we kept finding qualified candidates who happened to be women. Each got the job because we felt she was the best candidate we interviewed.

In some industries, being a woman can be quite an advantage. Women naturally tend to demonstrate higher ratings in certain traits and skills than men. This phenomenon didn't occur to me until the facts were right under my nose. I was your typical male manager who considered the women who worked for me to be very effective, but not as consistently effective as men. I just naturally expected the guys in the sales organization to win sales contests and to have the highest levels of achievement. I was biased. But I was also a believer in the science of sales. And the sales numbers didn't lie.

(continues)

(continued)

> The women on our sales team were competing head to head with the men. Then, two years in a row, a woman won the coveted sales representative of the year award. Furthermore, fully half of the salespeople who earned a spot on the President's Council at our company were women. It didn't take me long to change my bias.

Women's Traits for Sales Success

What are some of the traits that are most often related to women—and how do these relate to a career in sales? They include the following:

- **Nurturing and caring.** Women seem more natural at raising families and staying close to friends. This kind of caring also translates into caring about customers. Customers can sense this.

- **Intuitive.** Many women are very aware and mindful of the emotions and intentions of the people they are interacting with. This enhanced ability leads to better "reading" of customers. The result is better communication with customers and a better understanding of their needs.

- **Organized and multi-tasking.** Perhaps because women often bear the task of managing a household as well as a job, many have developed exceptional organizational skills. And because they can manage multiple tasks at the same time, women in sales tend to be able to handle a lot of customers, problems, and opportunities very naturally. The result is a very efficient, high-capacity selling machine.

- **Detail-oriented.** Any woman who can handle multi-tasking has to pay attention to details. Women seem great at writing lists and going back over the list to take care of each item. Nothing drops through the cracks. This trait is essential in following up, following through, and delivering on promises made to customers.

- **Good conversationalists.** Women, especially moms, are used to dealing with a lot of different kinds of people on different levels.

Even if she's employed full time, often it is the woman in the family who takes on the job of interacting with school teachers, principals, volunteers, other children, other parents, doctors, nurses, and so forth. Women learn and become quite good at conversing on a wide variety of topics with many different people.

- **Relationship-building.** Who are the social organizers in most families? Who are the peacemakers and diplomats in most families? The women. They seem to naturally connect with other people and start communicating effortlessly. Add communicating and caring together and you have the roots of a relationship. Ted notes, "The women who worked for me had extremely close relationships with their customers and even prospective customers. They were always aware of important things going on at a customer's office such as birthdays, vacations, or illnesses, and they took the time to mark these special occasions in ways that were remembered by their customers."

- **Self-starting.** The chores have to get done and the family has to be taken care of. Women, especially mothers, are out of bed and on the job whether they're at home, at a business, or managing both at the same time. Women are born self-starters and hard workers.

- **Problem-solving.** Women clean up so many messes. Some messes are spilt milk or broken glass. Some messes are hurt feelings. Or it could be the bully down the block. Women seem to tackle problems head on. A mess they inherit with a customer will seem easy by comparison to the messes at home.

- **Non-threatening.** Finally, women don't threaten men and they don't seem to threaten each other. This is a big factor in women's success in sales. Most customers across many industries are men. When a man tries to sell to another man, you have something of a confrontation of egos. As you would learn in a Wilson Learning sales course, this confrontation causes a high tension level. When customers are in a state of high tension, their ability to constructively listen to the sales presentation is very low. This tension must be reduced. Women, on the other hand, typically don't create a high level of tension in male audiences. Men lower their defenses in the presence of a woman. They will listen more effectively to what she has to say.

It might take a male salesperson two or three separate sales appointments to get the tension level with a male customer down to a point that the customer will finally really hear what the salesman has to say. In the meantime, a saleswoman might have achieved the same results in one sales call. Is this universal? Of course not. At the same time, women overall seem to be able to communicate with each other with less tension. Sometimes this is out of mutual respect and natural camaraderie. So a personable saleswoman will have an advantage whether she is dealing with men or women.

Put all these advantages together in a motivated, well-trained woman and the result will be sales success. These traits are particularly advantageous in industries with a high level of relationship selling.

Successful Women in Sales: Nine Portraits

We interviewed nine women who have built successful sales careers. Although we found no tried-and-true "formula" for getting into the field, we were able to identify several themes and trends that point to sustained success:

- **It helps to be outgoing.** Over and over, our interviewees told us, "You have to really like people." Talking and listening to customers helps you determine what their needs are. And if you enjoy getting to know new people, you'll find cold-calling less intimidating.

- **Good training is invaluable.** Good instincts and natural abilities are important but will take you only so far. The best companies train their salespeople in the sales process, and following the process leads to success.

- **Sell what you love.** Your passion for your product or service will propel you past the obstacles and challenges as you get started in your career.

- **The customer is king.** In the vignettes that follow, you'll read tale after tale of these women going out of their way to serve their customers. You can't do it just because you expect a payback; but you'll find it's a habit that will reward you repeatedly throughout your career.

As you read through these stories of women in sales, think about your situation, talents, and career experiences. You could be writing your own successful sales story if you follow the examples of these outstanding professionals!

- Advertising (Dawn Schaeffer)

- Automobiles (Lori Martin)

- Insurance and investments (Amy McPike)

- Freight services (Bonnie Knoedler)

- Meetings and events (Gale Santacreu)

- Pharmaceuticals (Charlotte Alden)

- Real Estate (Sue Smith)

- Skin Care and Image Services (Marcia Dever)

- Women's Apparel (LeAnn Nelson)

Dawn Schaeffer—Advertising (Professional Health Care Publishing)

POSITION: Regional Sales Manager, Boucher Communications
EDUCATION: Bachelor's degree in marketing, minor in management
YEARS IN SALES: 5
POSITION PRIOR TO SALES: Production manager for Boucher Communications

It took nine months for Dawn to get her boss at Boucher to give her a chance in sales. At first her boss complained, "What will I do without you? You are the best production manager I've ever had." Dawn's reply was, "What makes you think I can't be the best sales rep you've ever had?" Over those nine months she handled her campaign like a sales pro. She kept in touch with her boss and upper management about the sales job that might open up. At the same time, she worked hard at the job she had and did everything to the best of her ability.

When considering the most important traits for success in sales, Dawn says, "You must have an outgoing personality and you have to take rejection well." And what does she love about sales? "Travel, meeting different people, and making good money."

For Dawn the shift into sales wasn't difficult. "It wasn't hard for me at all. I have the personality for it. From the time I started working after college, many supervisors and co-workers have said, 'You should be in sales.'" And they were right. In terms of market share, she leads her colleagues with the highest ranking.

Dawn shares her most interesting sales experience to date. "The readership and integrity of my magazine were being challenged by one of my clients. His information was based on misleading statistics provided to him by a dishonest competitor. I was in deep jeopardy of losing about $35,000 in business from this client who had in the past been a big supporter of our magazine. At first, I was defensive and angry, but I quickly realized that this attitude would get me nowhere. After going into my publisher's office and exploding, I composed myself and got every bit of statistical information I could about our magazine's status and strengths. I faxed this to the client and called him 30 minutes later to calmly and clearly discuss this more accurate information. I focused on the success this client had had with our magazine and how the focus of our magazine was the most appropriate for his company. After a lengthy phone call, he agreed to keep his advertising dollars with me. I consider this a success. Fortunately, this is not an everyday experience."

Dawn has the following advice for those considering a career in sales: "One, you must be outgoing and driven to succeed. No sales rep was ever successful waiting for the business to come to them. Two, a professional image is essential if you want to be taken seriously. And three, no limp handshake…EVER."

Lori Martin—Automobiles

POSITION: Client Advisor, The BMW Store
YEARS IN SALES: 15
EDUCATION: B.S. in marketing
OCCUPATION PRIOR TO SALES: None
PRIOR TO CURRENT POSITION: High-end women's clothing sales and store management

Lori sold *herself* into her current position. When the specialty women's clothing store she managed went out of business, she thought about her skills, interests, and abilities and decided that another high-end product was just what she wanted to sell. Zeroing in on BMW automobiles, she picked up the phone, called the general manager of the dealership, and was able to wangle a meeting. "I had to convince him a bit," she says, "but I kept calling back." That persistence resulted in her being hired for a position where she's had great success, quickly reaching "Charter" level (sales of more than 100 cars per year) by her second year.

Lori always knew she wanted to be in sales and pursued a sales job right out of college. She loves the variety—"it's different every day and has a low boredom factor!" Her advice to people interested in sales is to sell something that you love. Your interest and passion will communicate themselves to your customers, and you'll have a great deal of job satisfaction as well as success.

BMW provides extensive sales training, and in fact Lori's dealership prefers to bring in salespeople without automotive sales experience. For the first six months on the job, she learned everything she could about BMW vehicles. That solid product knowledge, combined with her existing sales abilities, made her transition fairly smooth.

Lori believes the most important traits for people going into sales are an outgoing personality, persistence (a "never-give-up" attitude), and a sense of fun and enjoyment in the job. She doesn't believe in high-pressure sales tactics, but stresses the importance of good listening skills to find out what the customer really wants. Sometimes what they want isn't what they first tell you, and a good salesperson will be flexible and open-minded to the customer's spoken and unspoken needs. That might result in a much larger sale and will always result in greater customer satisfaction.

Amy McPike—Insurance and Investments

POSITION: Financial Representative, Northwestern Mutual Financial Network
YEARS IN SALES: 12
EDUCATION: Bachelor's degree in finance
POSITION PRIOR TO SALES: Commercial banking lender

"Sell something you're passionate about!" is Amy's advice to women considering sales as a career. She herself took that advice when she transitioned from a career in banking to her current position helping individuals and businesses by developing financial solutions that fit their needs throughout their lifecycles. Amy not only believes in the products and services she sells, she gets great satisfaction from problem-solving for her clients and helping them progress toward their financial goals.

As a financial representative, Amy essentially runs her own business. She is responsible for establishing and achieving her own goals (her compensation is 100 percent commission-based), setting her own hours, and prioritizing her activities so that she is getting the necessary tasks done but devoting most of her time to meeting with clients and prospects. She stresses that it's essential for salespeople to understand their own individual strengths—"and don't be afraid to look for help in filling whatever gaps you might have." Amy has an assistant who manages the organizational facets of her job, and she often partners with other specialists during various parts of the sales process.

Amy also advises sales professionals to really understand what their market is. Her clients are primarily individuals and small businesses, and although at times she's participated in large sales to big companies, she is careful to keep her efforts focused on her "bread-and-butter" clients. She once lost sight of her key market and spent more than a year cultivating a large corporate client—only to be dismayed when the company chose not to purchase. That decision meant a tough year for Amy, but it also helped her to refocus on her core business. She's been going strong ever since!

Northwestern Mutual Financial Network offers an excellent training program. Amy completed several weeks of company-sponsored training, and for the next three years she enjoyed a formal support system and an enhanced commission program that helped her launch her business on a solid footing.

Amy believes firmly in identifying and meeting clients' needs instead of just "pushing products." This approach is one of the keys to her success—and a big reason why she's built a loyal client base and a steady, successful business.

Amy is an agent of the Northwestern Mutual Life Insurance Company, Milwaukee, Wisconsin.

Bonnie Knoedler—Freight Services

POSITION: Sales Executive, AdCom Worldwide
YEARS IN SALES: 20
EDUCATION: Bachelor's degree
POSITION PRIOR TO SALES: Part-time retail sales while in college
PRIOR TO CURRENT POSITION: Telemarketer

Getting into sales wasn't difficult for Bonnie. "I have always felt I had sales in my blood," she says. She convinced AdCom during her first four months as a trainee and telemarketer. Over the phone she produced a lot of very good appointments for the sales executives. This proved to the management that she should be given a sales executive position. Since then she has won almost every award that the company has ever offered. She has been told that she is the top sales executive throughout the company's 30 offices.

The things Bonnie loves about sales are the people she deals with, the daily challenges of the industry, and the new things she continues to learn. She will tell you that the most important trait in sales is confidence; the most important skill is knowledge. And the advice she would give someone considering a sales career is "to stay highly motivated regardless of the letdowns. Don't take things personally. Learn the product or service inside and out. Do not be afraid to ask for help and advice." She concludes by saying. "Anyone coming into sales as a 'know-it-all' will not succeed."

One of Bonnie's early sales experiences taught her a valuable lesson. "When I started here, 17 years ago, my boss decided to hand me an account, a law firm. They were shipping estate files to a gentleman in Chicago who was on his deathbed. We shipped the boxes via a major air carrier and they lost them. I had to be the one to let the client know of the lost boxes. It was very overwhelming for me at this novice stage of my career. The airline did end up finding the boxes in time to reach the gentleman before he succumbed, but the pressure was really on. That experience taught me to be honest and to provide lots of communication with the client. This has become one of my mottos."

Gale Santacreu—Meetings and Events

POSITION: National Sales Manager, Audio Visual Innovations, Creative Show Services Division
YEARS IN SALES: 20
EDUCATION: Some college
OCCUPATION PRIOR TO SALES: Hotel Food and Beverage Management
PRIOR TO CURRENT POSITION: Banquet sales

"I sell an experience," says Gale. And, depending on the client, the experience might be designed for one hundred or several thousand people. These experiences include huge stage sets and computerized lighting and light shows for corporate meetings. For any one client she will sell and then coordinate a video production, custom stage design, specialty lighting and effects, state-of-the-art audiovisual equipment, celebrity entertainment, and full event management. If it means creating a grand entrance by having the CEO start the meeting by riding in on an elephant or in a Range Rover with live tigers, so be it! Gale wasn't looking for a sales job when she was offered one. "I was talked into it." she laughs. "And it was my first lesson in listening." A manager from another hotel asked her to leave her job as a restaurant manager to become his banquet sales manager. He told her that he knew she would be successful. After initially resisting, she accepted and launched her career in sales. After 11 years in hotel catering sales, she transitioned into meeting and event sales. She credits the hospitality industry with a willingness to send salespeople to a variety of training programs. The first hotels she worked for all sent her to very good sales-training courses.

Gale's favorite things about selling are the excitement of getting the sale, the friendly relationships she makes, having fun, and seeing the satisfaction on her clients' faces when they see what her production team has created for them. "I just love to see their faces when they walk in the room," she says. Prior to the actual show, the clients have seen only artist renderings of what they are paying for.

The four most important traits/skills in selling, according to Gale, are good listening skills, passion about the product or service you are selling, caring about your clients, and having fun selling. Her advice to someone new to sales is to have integrity. If you are considering sales, she recommends getting a full-time or part-time job right in the middle of the sales activity at a company. Then see if you like it.

Charlotte Alden*—Pharmaceuticals

POSITION: District Sales Manager for a major pharmaceutical firm
YEARS IN SALES: 10
EDUCATION: B.S. in finance
OCCUPATION PRIOR TO SALES: Corporate finance
PRIOR TO CURRENT POSITION: Managed Care Account Manager

*Name has been fictionalized.

"For me, sales was a whole new ballgame," says Charlotte, who transitioned from finance to gain a broader understanding of her company's products. "But once I learned the rules and decided I wanted to play the game, I played to win!"

That competitive drive has been a key to Charlotte's success as she has won numerous sales awards and advanced through three sales positions to her current level of District Sales Manager for a groundbreaking new drug. "When I discovered the freedom and independence, the control I had over my activities and results, I found that sales was a better fit for my personality."

A challenging lesson she learned was to use "situational leadership"—to be versatile and vary her approach depending on the personality, style, and needs of her customer. One of her greatest success stories resulted from her ability to recover from a mistake ("I annoyed the most important customer in my territory when I was brand-new on the job"). Through persistence and frank communication, she was able to regain her customer's trust and build an exceptionally strong relationship.

Now that she is responsible for managing a sales team, when she is recruiting new salespeople Charlotte looks for competitive drive, great relationship-building skills, persistence, and—a key attribute in her field—strong technical competency. "If they don't have a background in pharmaceutical sales, I ask them technical questions about other areas of their experience. I look at their academic record to see how well they were able to learn technical information in a variety of areas. They need to know our products and competitors and have the confidence to go toe-to-toe with a highly educated customer."

Charlotte finds it very rewarding to work in a field where she is able to improve people's health and well-being. She stresses that you must have sales goals and understand that your job is to sell, but to achieve sustained results it is essential to keep the patient in mind every day on the job.

Sue Smith—Residential Real Estate

POSITION: Senior Sales Consultant, Empire Realty Associates
YEARS IN REAL-ESTATE SALES: 16
EDUCATION: Bachelor's degree in organizational behavior
PRIOR TO CURRENT POSITION: District Manager, American Express Travel and Financial Services

Sue started selling when she was 16 years old, working at a clothing store in Oakland, California. She was supposed to sell only clothes, but she did so well that she was allowed to sell furs, too. The experience at the clothing store set Sue on the sales career track at an early age. Altogether, she has been in sales for more than 40 years.

Prior to selling real estate, Sue was the district manager for American Express Travel and Financial Services—in fact, she was named one of the top managers for American Express in the United States. She specialized in marketing and sales promotions. One year, her small team was ranked number one in the U.S. for selling Hawaiian vacations and other travel products. One of the things she did was sell incentive programs for real-estate companies. In 1986, she filled an entire cruise ship with real-estate agents who had won the trip due to their outstanding sales performance. This is one of her favorite stories. Not only did she fill a ship with 750 people, but she helped the captain and purser plan exactly what program and activities to present the entire time of the cruise.

In real estate, Sue consistently ranks in the top two percent of Realtors nationwide. She has always been one of the top 10 salespeople in any office where she has worked. She loves selling real estate because she loves houses, selling, and the interesting variety of people she gets to work with. One of those people was Ted. What Ted remembers is Sue's willingness to invest in a customer and then her persistence later. First, Sue helped Ted find a home to rent. Obviously, this wasn't a deal that was going to make her a lot of money. However, that didn't matter to Sue. She put the same effort into helping Ted with a rental property as she did in selling a house. Two years later, this effort on her part paid off as she helped Ted purchase a home. Then, when it was time to sell his home, an interesting thing happened. Ted tried to sell it himself. Although Ted is an excellent medical sales executive, he isn't a real-estate sales expert. For two months and numerous open houses, nothing happened. During this period, Sue professionally and persistently offered advice and expressed her willingness to sell the house. She could have taken a negative attitude, but she didn't. She persisted. Finally, Ted said, "Sue, you do it." Sue put the marketing power of her real-estate company together with her sales skills and had the house sold in three days from the time it was listed.

For someone considering real-estate sales, Sue says it is important to commit the first several years to learning the business and establishing your name in the community. She continues, "It will take time and money—money to live on while you wait for your first commission checks. Also, a new real-estate agent must have the ability to put all technologies to use—things such as cell phones, digital cameras, computers, and faxes." Sue found many of her first clients by holding open houses for properties on weekends. She put in the "grunt work" to build a client base, and then she worked hard to maintain her client relationships to generate repeat business and referrals.

"I think someone with persistence, the ability to control clients, and good organizational skills will do well in real estate," says Sue. She continues, "Even though you will start out working for a real-estate company, you are still your own boss, so you must be self-motivated."

Obviously, Sue has worked according to the advice she has given. She continues to be successful selling real estate and recently joined with several other agents to open an independent brokerage in Danville, California.

Marcia Dever—Skin Care and Image Services (Direct Sales)

POSITION: Executive Director and Independent Consultant, BeautiControl
YEARS IN SALES: 18

EDUCATION: B.A. from Georgetown University (Kentucky) and
M.S. from University of Virginia
POSITION PRIOR TO SALES: Elementary and middle-school
teacher
PRIOR TO CURRENT POSITION: Consultant, Director

"The last thing I ever expected was to be in sales!" says Marcia, looking back on a very successful 18-year career with BeautiControl. Advancing from part-time consultant through director and senior-director levels, she now manages a business with seven directors and nearly 600 consultants nationwide.

Because growth in the business is built on recruiting new consultants, Marcia has extensive experience evaluating candidates' potential for success in sales. Sales experience is not a requirement. She looks for two primary traits: people skills and a positive attitude. "You have to love people and you have to be an optimist. I've seen people you would least expect really grow and blossom when given the chance."

BeautiControl does offer initial and ongoing sales training. Consultants set their own sales goals and can work as many hours as they want, but advancement to director level and beyond requires meeting stringent company-set goals for sales revenue and sales-team recruitment.

Marcia's sales performance is in the top-third of her peer group of about 80 Executive Directors nationwide. She has won many performance awards such as diamond jewelry and first-class trips to luxury vacation spots. She reports that her husband jumped on board with full-fledged support once he enjoyed a trip to Hawaii that Marcia won for her sales results—although that seemed like an impossible goal at her first sales presentation. She had closed the presentation by saying, "You don't have to buy a thing." Her confidence was also shaken by some early parties, where she competed with dogs and children to get the attention of customers. Her advice to people getting into sales: "Be persistent, be consistent, be determined."

LeAnn Nelson—Women's Apparel (Direct Sales)

POSITION: Independent Sales Manager, Weekenders USA, Inc.
YEARS IN SALES: 20
EDUCATION: B.S. in dietetics, University of Texas at Austin
POSITION PRIOR TO SALES: Retail store owner/manager
PRIOR TO CURRENT POSITION: Cosmetics sales

LeAnn has been successful in diverse fields throughout her career, so it's no surprise that she flourished when she entered direct sales and subsequently advanced to sales management. In fact, she thinks "adaptability" is one of her strongest traits and one that is essential in the field of sales. She transitioned from dietitian to public-relations representative to owning her own store. Then, faced with the increasingly competitive retail market for women's accessories, she conducted a thorough assessment of her strengths, weaknesses, and interests to find a new, more satisfying, and more lucrative field. That assessment led her to develop a career as an author and speaker on the topic of women's accessories. Searching for products to promote in addition to her own book, she learned about direct-sales opportunities with Mary Kay cosmetics. For 10 years she ran a successful, profitable Mary Kay business that gave her the flexibility she needed to care for her aging mother. Just three years ago, she was enticed by a networking contact to take a look at Weekenders, and a year later she discontinued selling Mary Kay and devoted her full energies to building the Weekenders business.

About a year ago, LeAnn took on a new challenge—that of sales manager. She built her business by sponsoring new fashion coordinators and achieving company-set minimums for sales volume. Now, having expanded her unit to 24 sales coordinators, she leads monthly sales meetings and helps her team work together to meet individual and group goals. LeAnn is one of about 370 sales managers for Weekenders, a fast-growing company with 15,000 independent representatives nationwide.

LeAnn believes that there are tremendous opportunities for women in direct-sales companies such as Weekenders, Mary Kay, and

BeautiControl; these positions give women the opportunity to work part- or full-time, combine work with family care, and generate substantial income. It's important to affiliate with a reputable company, and LeAnn recommends researching company financials, growth trends, and affiliation with industry organizations such as the Direct Selling Association.

When asked about traits she looks for in sales recruits, LeAnn says that it's essential they be able to operate independently, have the discipline to work from home without being distracted, be goal oriented, and have an outgoing personality. LeAnn gets tremendous satisfaction from helping other women build their own successful businesses and sees exciting growth ahead for her company, herself, and her sales team.

Wrap-up and To Do

We're not saying that because you're a woman you're guaranteed to have a successful sales career. Nor are we saying that men can't rise to the top in sales. Both statements would be ridiculous! But we do believe that women, because of the strength of their inherent traits, have advantages that can make them phenomenal salespeople.

It makes sense to consider all of your strengths when you're considering a career move. Be aware of them and use them to your advantage. Don't dismiss certain skills or traits because you've used them only at home or in a volunteer position. Instead, take a realistic look at all of the traits we've outlined in this chapter and in chapter 5 and see how you can use them to your advantage in your sales career.

CHAPTER 7 Strategies for Breaking Into Sales

After studying the pros and cons, carefully assessing your skills and character traits, and learning what it's really like to be in sales, you've decided that this is the career for you. Great! Whether you're just out of college or making a mid-career transition, in this chapter you'll learn how to sell yourself as a strong candidate for the jobs you're interested in.

That's right—the first sales challenge of your new career will be to position and market *yourself.* First you must get the attention of decision makers, then present yourself as the solution to their needs, and finally close the deal for your new position. That's what any job search is all about, so those who have an inherent understanding of "how to sell" have a leg up on the competition right from the start.

As you read through this chapter, you'll find an opening section on choosing a specific area of sales for your first position, whether you're starting out with no experience or are transitioning from another career into sales at either the mid or senior level. Then we'll walk you through developing your strategy and creating an important tool to make the transition: your resume.

As you might imagine, resume-writing strategies for starting or transitioning into a new field differ from those used by people who are advancing in the same field. In their cases, their work history shows relevant experience and is a clear indicator of their career interests. But if you want to move from tech support to sales, or pet care to sales, or training to sales management, you'll have to use a different strategy. This chapter will tell you how, show you examples, and finish with a worksheet you can use for developing your own resume.

Where the Jobs Are: Strategy and Industry Recommendations

Before you can create your *sales strategy*—a plan for how you'll get from where you are to where you want to be—it's important to narrow down the field of "sales" into one or a few specific areas. Throughout this book, as you've read stories about successful salespeople, you've probably noticed that their backgrounds and areas of expertise are quite different from one another, as are the products they sell and the way they sell them. Perhaps you're interested in one of these areas or have ideas for entirely different industries in which you'd like to specialize. To give you some more food for thought, we've compiled lists of industries and grouped them into general categories according to where you are in your career—entry-level career starter or mid- or senior-level career transitioner. Education and some other factors are also considered.

Of course, these groupings are not absolute. We know people who have broken into competitive sales positions against all odds and have been tremendously successful. But we also know people who set their sights on an unrealistic goal and then gave up when they couldn't achieve it easily. It's important to be persistent yet realistic in pursuing your aspiration.

Entry-Level Strategies

It might seem illogical, but it's usually easier to enter the field of sales if you have *no* experience than if you've worked in other fields and want to switch to sales. That's because employers hiring entry-level salespeople typically look for traits and characteristics (as discussed in chapter 5) rather than expertise in sales or knowledge of a particular product or industry. Key factors for selection also include education and academic achievement. Later in the chapter we discuss how to use your resume to indicate that you have the key attributes the employer is looking for.

Best Industries for College Graduates with a 3.0 or Higher GPA or Master's Degree

The following areas of sales are the most competitive—they pay well, are highly sought after, and usually have the most stringent qualifications for entry. Some companies in these fields have strict requirements for college GPA, and they might adhere to this requirement even several years after you've graduated and even if you have successful sales experience in another field. For these reasons, we want you to be realistic about your ability to land a job in this field unless you have at least a 3.0 GPA. A high GPA indicates not only intelligence, but also the discipline to apply intelligence to your studies. The reason these top-tier companies are so successful is that they pick the best people to work for them. You can understand that a medical device company wants a smart person explaining the use of a surgical instrument or device to a surgeon.

- Pharmaceuticals

- Medical devices

- Financial services—top-tier companies

- Industrial products that fit your field of study (for instance, industrial chemicals for a chemical-engineering graduate)

- Blue-chip corporations (IBM, Johnson & Johnson, Procter & Gamble)

- Software or hardware

Best Industries for College Graduates with an Average or Less-Than-Average GPA

The following industries also offer excellent sales opportunities and satisfying careers. Because they are slightly less competitive than the first-tier companies and industries mentioned in the preceding section, they offer greater opportunity to the average student. Even poor students can land jobs in these industries, provided that you are able to demonstrate the key qualities and characteristics necessary for success in sales.

- Financial services—second-tier companies
- Consumer technology products
- Media advertising
- Telecommunications services
- Industrial products
- Transportation

Best Industries for People with No College Degree

Some of the companies and industries shown in this category offer the equivalent of self-employment, such as home sales and manufacturers' representatives. Others typically employ salespeople without college degrees. Still others, such as some office-products companies, are willing to hire just about anyone who has the basic characteristics for success. There is rapid turnover and often little support with these companies, but they know that true salespeople will be successful. And if you are successful in such a high-pressure environment, you will build a great foundation from which you can step into another, more prestigious sales position. Some of the jobs in this category, such as real estate sales, require specific training or certification before you are eligible to sell.

- Industrial or consumer-goods products sold via manufacturers' representatives firms
- Packaged foods
- Office equipment such as copiers and faxes
- Real estate
- Cosmetics

■ Home-sales products (such as Mary Kay, Pampered Chef, and BeautiControl)

Strategies for Mid-Career Transition

You have some experience under your belt but have decided that sales is a better fit for your skills and interests than what you're doing now. To get that first sales position, you can take one of four approaches:

1. Consider yourself an "entry-level" salesperson, minimize your unrelated experience, and follow the same recommendations as described in the preceding section.

2. Use the expertise you've gained as "added value" for the company that hires you to sell its products or services. If you choose this option, do some brainstorming to develop a list of potential businesses and industries that would be interested in your knowledge. These might include the following:

   ■ Your current company

   ■ Key competitors of your current company

   ■ Your company's suppliers

   ■ Your company's customers

   ■ Companies that sell to the same customer base as yours

   ■ Companies that buy from the same supplier base

3. Make a two-step transition. This will work if you are running into resistance at your company in regard to your ability to move into sales. Offer to take a sales-support role. Some companies have a number of different people who assist with sales. For example, a high-tech company might have field engineers who work with the salespeople. An office-products company has its equipment service people. Any opportunity to mix with the sales organization and with customers will help move you in the right direction. Then look for opportunities to move into a sales position.

4. Offer to take the most demanding customers or the most poorly performing territory. Here you are offering the company an opportunity to reduce its risk in hiring you. By taking the worst customers or worst territory, you are acknowledging the company's concern about hiring an inexperienced sales representative. You are showing the initiative and courage to take on a difficult challenge. And you might be solving a problem for them.

When it comes time to write your resume, be sure to position your industry expertise and "insider" knowledge as a key selling point. You'll read more about this later in the chapter.

Senior-Level Transition Strategies

This is probably the most difficult transition into sales. You've reached a certain level in your career and have an enormous amount of expertise. But you might also have high expectations about compensation, seniority, and title. On the other hand, even if you're willing to move down several levels, hiring companies might not see what advantages you offer over a younger, more malleable individual just starting a career. We recommend one of two approaches:

1. Use strategy #2 in the preceding section as outlined for mid-level career changers. You too can position yourself as a valuable expert who can help a company enter a new market or oust key competitors. After all, you have years of experience and countless contacts in your industry. The trick to positioning yourself is to downplay experience that is unrelated to your sales goal and to be sure not to convey too much of a "senior" level of expertise that could make companies shy away from what they perceive to be the high cost of hiring you.

2. Look for opportunities within your own company, where you're known and respected. Ask for a part-time assignment in sales, an expansion of your current role to include sales, or a senior sales executive as a mentor. You might not be able to transition into 100 percent sales, but you should get the chance to add some components of sales to your job—and do so without losing

compensation, level, or status. Eventually, if you still strongly desire a full-time sales role, you can position your new sales experience as part of the highlights of your qualifications as you look for a new position either inside or outside your company.

Use the worksheets at the end of this chapter to create your target industry lists. You'll refine and narrow your choices throughout the networking and interviewing process as you find the right opportunity.

The Dale Carnegie Course as a Proving Ground

If you have no experience in sales, yet are trying to transition into this career, how can you prove to yourself and a potential employer that you are capable of selling? One recommendation is to take the Dale Carnegie Course. Dale Carnegie is a highly regarded training company that offers a large selection of courses. These courses are good for anyone whether or not they are interested in sales. However, individuals who succeed in the original Dale Carnegie Course do so because they demonstrate sales-oriented traits and skills. Also, they quickly and enthusiastically learn the skills that the Dale Carnegie courses teach. Dale Carnegie also offers a sales course called Sales Advantage. Both of these courses are offered in the evenings, so they won't interfere with your current job.

If you take one of these courses and like it, it is a good indication that you will be comfortable in a sales environment. Furthermore, it is proof to a potential employer that your interest in sales is not a whim. The employer will see that you took the initiative to take the course at your own expense. The experience will give you additional confidence in your ability to step out of the career box you have been in up to this point. This confidence will show in any interview you have for a sales position. Finally, it is something that you can put on your resume.

Be sure to ask your current employer if they will reimburse you for taking one of these courses. You might be pleasantly surprised by the answer. Many companies will reimburse employees for all or part of the cost of courses. When asking, present the brochure to your superior and explain what you expect to get out of the course and how it will benefit you and the company. Don't be disappointed if your boss says, "No." Take the course as an investment you are making in yourself.

Ted tells this story as proof positive of the effectiveness of this approach:

> *Years ago, I was asked about sales jobs by a woman who worked in another department of my company. Her husband, who worked in our manufacturing area, had accepted a transfer to our plant in Texas. She wanted to try to get a job in sales after moving to Texas, but she had no sales experience. I suggested the Dale Carnegie course. She took my advice. She loved the course. Upon arriving in Texas, she immediately got a sales-oriented job at a bank. She told me later that the advice to take the course made all the difference. It gave her confidence to pursue something different.*

Another great organization to join is Toastmasters, where you'll have the opportunity to learn and practice public speaking in a competitive yet supportive environment. You'll improve your presentation ability, build your self-confidence, and show employers that you are serious about learning better sales skills.

Contact information for Dale Carnegie, Toastmasters, and other organizations is listed in the appendix.

Why Companies Hire

To make yourself an attractive candidate for any position with any company, you must first understand why companies hire and what they look for in the people they consider. **Companies hire to fill a need or solve a problem.** In sales, the fundamental need is to generate revenue (sales dollars). But companies also often address additional needs when they hire people. These might include the following:

- Increasing their share of the market in a particular product or market segment

- Replacing competitors in key target accounts

- Introducing a new product or entering a new market

- Delivering exceptional service to a key account or group of accounts

- Taking advantage of a sudden market opportunity

In addition, the company might be experiencing some problems that it wants the new salesperson to solve, such as the following:

- Improving relationships and building sales in a neglected territory

- Fighting off competition in a small market or narrow customer base

- Improving the professional image of its sales force (and thus the company)

- Filling a job with a lot of "turnover"—where people are hired but don't stay long

- Filling jobs to rapidly expand in a given market

Before constructing your "sales pitch" (your resume, cover letter, and interview preparation), do what you can to find out about the needs of the particular company for the particular job you're seeking. In many cases you can learn about these needs and problems by talking to people who work at the company or are knowledgeable about the industry. You should also research the companies and industries in which you're interested. The Internet and your local library are great sources of information. (Check the appendix for some resources to get you started.) The more you learn, the better you'll be able to show that you are a solution for the company—that you know its challenges and can help solve its problems.

Selling Yourself in Your Resume and Cover Letter

Clearly we can't address all the nuances and complexities of writing a resume and cover letter in this one section of the book. Our goal is to highlight a general strategy and address some specific concerns you might have as you put together your first sales resume. If you need more help, we suggest that you consult a professional resume writer (see the resources in the appendix for a link to a directory of professional resume writers) or check your bookstore or library for one of the many excellent publications that cover this topic in depth. (Louise's book, *Sales and Marketing Resumes for $100,000 Careers*, also published by JIST, is a comprehensive resource and is applicable even if you're just starting out in sales.)

General Strategy

Your resume must be more than just a listing of your education credentials and work experience. It must convey that you have the *skills* and *traits* that are indicative of success in sales. Be sure to read chapter 5 to get a full understanding of these skills and traits and to assess the strength and balance of your own qualifications.

Equally important for an effective resume, you can't simply *state* that you have skills and abilities; you must prove it by including "success stories" that show how you've demonstrated them in the past. These stories can come from any area of your life, such as school, work, volunteer activities, sports, and extracurricular activities. In fact, if you're making a career transition, you might find that your role as director of Girl Scout cookie sales is more valuable on your resume than your full-time job as an accountant.

Your success stories—also known as achievements or accomplishments—are the most valuable part of your resume. Here's where you "put your money where your mouth is"; here's where you give employers a picture of a real reason and convince them that you can be successful in a sales job for their company.

There are many ways to organize and arrange the information on your resume. Follow the guidelines in the next sections to be sure you're emphasizing the most important information, projecting the right image for your current career goal, and making it as easy as possible for readers to absorb what you want them to learn about you in a quick glance. At the end of this chapter are worksheets to help you organize your information before writing your resume and cover letters.

Start Off with a Strong Summary

Resumes today often do not include an "Objective" statement. An Objective statement can be limiting because, to be meaningful, it must be quite specific. But for career changers or new graduates, an Objective is often a helpful focusing statement for readers. Whether or not you choose to use one, be sure to summarize your key attributes and qualifications at the top of the resume, along with some "reason to believe" evidence. Here are two sample summaries, one for a new graduate who worked part-time sales jobs through high school and college, and one for a social worker who has decided to change to a career in sales.

Sales Professional
Solution-Focused ■ **Customer-Oriented** ■ **Creative** ■ **Organized & Efficient**

- **Sales Qualifications:** Five-year track record of success in sales. Proven ability to identify needs and recommend solutions, build rapport, cross-sell, and manage post-sales follow-up.

- **Management & Leadership:** Talent for inspiring sales and customer-service staff to strive for excellence. Successfully managed sales, retail operations, purchasing, and customer service—with strong results in every position.

- **Communication & Conflict Resolution:** Effective as a mentor, trainer, staff manager, and handler of escalated customer-service issues.

- **Time Management & Organization:** Demonstrated ability to prioritize multiple roles and tasks to meet deadlines and achieve goals.

CAREER GOAL	SALES
SUMMARY OF QUALIFICATIONS	• **Communication skills:** persuasive and effective communicator… excellent listener… able to identify needs and develop solutions
	• **Degree in psychology:** both theoretical and practical understanding of human behavior and motivators
	• **Presentation & training abilities:** professional and focused in presenting recommendations to clients, colleagues, and employers… track record of effectively training disabled clients to become successful employees
	• **Problem-solving skills:** creative, persistent, and resourceful… able to help clients overcome barriers by brainstorming and problem-solving to resolve extremely diverse issues
	• **Planning, goal-setting, organization, & follow-through:** strong fundamental skills and ability to guide projects from start to finish

Include Only Relevant Information in Your Experience Section

If you worked as a retail sales manager but now want a job in direct sales, highlight the sales results your associates achieved under your direction; don't waste a lot of space describing your inventory-management experience or financial skills. If your experience was as a computer programmer, include only enough technical information to convey the expertise that will make you a good software salesperson—don't distract the reader with so much jargon that your resume shouts "techie" rather than "salesperson." And if your work history consists of part-time jobs in food service or yard maintenance, you might not need to include any details other than a bare-bones listing.

The following sample experience section shows how a training director focused her experience to highlight only sales-related activities to support her goal of a position as an account manager.

Experience and Accomplishments

MANAGEMENT SOLUTIONS, Oakbrook, IL	2002–Present

Director of Training

Joined start-up consulting firm that develops and presents programs to address pressing business issues. Initial focus is on raising visibility in the business community and promoting the company's two sales-training programs.

> ➤ Effectively built presence in the Chicago market through networking and business-development activities.

> ➤ Developed leads and built relationships that resulted in $50K sales revenue within first month on the job. Succeeded in gaining access to decision-makers at target companies.

> ➤ Co-led telemarketing skills training program, presenting sales concepts to diverse corporate clients with widely varying levels of skill and experience.

Think Outside the Box

Look at all of your diverse experiences to find evidence of your skills. Because your work experience might not be a primary qualifier as you seek a new type of career, the things you've done outside work become more important. Keep in mind the traits and abilities that indicate success in sales (discussed in depth in chapter 5), and examine your activities and involvements for evidence of those qualities. Did you manage a soccer team to a regional championship? That shows good leadership, teamwork, and communication skills. Did you persuade 50 people to join a campus society? Clearly that shows the ability to influence people and move them to action.

To secure a position selling Harley-Davidson motorcycles, the individual whose resume excerpt follows emphasized his Harley activities rather than his "real" job in administrative management—in fact, that experience didn't even appear until page 2 of his resume.

RELEVANT EXPERIENCE

Massachusetts State HOG Rally Committee   2002
SITE COORDINATOR
Worked collaboratively with coordinators from 3 cities to execute highly successful statewide touring event. Managed all Worcester-area program elements: Selected venues, planned activities, and recruited and led 25-member team of volunteers throughout 7-month planning period and 3-day event.

- Recruited by Harley Regional Manager to step in mid-stream and manage event to completion.
- As part of Rally Central Committee, set policies and made decisions for the event.
- Attracted strong and enthusiastic participation—resulting in the largest touring rally (state or national) ever sponsored by Harley-Davidson.

Harley Owners Group—Central Massachusetts Chapter, Worcester, MA   1999–Present
DIRECTOR, 2001–Present
ASSISTANT DIRECTOR, 1999–2001
Charter member and active leader of 150-member owners group. Develop strategic plans and membership-building programs; lead executive team in planning and coordinating 3–4 member events monthly.

- Launched incentive program that boosted member participation 5% within months of implementation.
- Participated in annual Harley-sponsored officer-training programs.

Don't Confine Yourself to a Traditional Chronological Format

If you're making a career transition from lawyer to salesperson, readers of your resume might find it hard to look past your 10 years of experience as a law-firm associate. So don't make it easy for them to focus in on this information. Instead, consider separating your achievements from your experience so that you sell yourself with the most relevant information first.

The following sample shows a substantial "Career Highlights" section for a business manager with diverse experience. Deciding he wanted to pursue a sales career, he pulled out the most compelling information and presented it "front and center" on his resume.

CAREER HIGHLIGHTS

◆ **Grew sales volume of independent travel agency from $500K to $2.1 million in 6 years**—solely responsible for sales strategy, marketing plans and materials, community outreach, and website marketing, all while serving in primary role as travel agent.

— Built business through innovative sales strategies, community marketing, referrals, and reputation for above-and-beyond service.

— Maintained excellent relationships with key carriers and travel service providers as well as with corporate accounts.

◆ **Increased sales revenue 15% annually** for home-services business in a competitive market.

— Took over underperforming business and improved profitability, morale, accountability, and communication while steadily increasing sales.

◆ **Negotiated contracts** and managed office relocation 3 times to more visible and more cost-effective sites.

— Developed negotiating strategy that tied our key priorities to specific circumstances of each rental property. Successful in gaining high-value concessions.

Put Together a Complete Picture

Based on the preceding examples, you can see how each section of your resume can—and should—display a consistent theme of sales-related attributes, activities, and achievements. Here are a few final tips for creating a high-powered resume that gets noticed and focuses attention where you want it:

- **Pay attention to format, layout, and overall appearance.** Strive for a professional, uncluttered look, and use appropriate formatting enhancements (such as bold type, italics, different font sizes, and graphic lines) to make it easy for the reader to pick up essential information quickly.

- **Don't get hung up on resume length.** Although one-page resumes are the norm for most new graduates, and two-page resumes are standard for people with 10 or more years of experience, don't worry if you don't fit these very general guidelines. It's more important that you say what you need to say, highlight the right information, and paint just the right picture than that you stay within some arbitrary page guideline. (Research shows that hiring authorities aren't at all concerned about resume length as long as the resume is interesting, relevant, well written, and well presented.)

- Be absolutely certain there are no typographical, grammatical, punctuation, or formatting errors on your resume. Don't let an employer's first impression of you be a negative one!

- **Be totally truthful.** Lying on your resume is not only easy for an employer to uncover (and subsequently dismiss you even after you've been hired), it is unethical—and unnecessary, if you take the time to identify and spotlight the value you have to offer. Keep in mind, however, that you can select the information you want to present—you don't have to tell everything. This is entirely ethical and appropriate; you're simply presenting the information that qualifies you for the positions you're seeking.

Sample Resumes for Sales Professionals

Take a look at the following sample resumes. They illustrate successful strategies for translating non-sales experience into sales qualifications. Some were written for new graduates with little practical experience; these highlight sales-related traits and skills, supported by evidence in the form of activities and achievements. Others, prepared for mid-career professionals, show how their extensive experience can be "mined" to find strong selling points for a sales position above the entry level.

CHRIS CANYON

25 Totoket Road, North Branford, CT 06471 • (203) 484-9054 • ChrisCanyon@hotmail.com

Qualified for MEDICAL or PHARMACEUTICAL SALES positions through:

- Proven sales abilities… consistent track record of outperforming sales goals
- Deep knowledge of hospital operations and medical procedures
- Expert ability to establish rapport with physicians and other health-care professionals
- Organizational, leadership, and persuasive communication skills

Professional Experience

HEALTH CARE **Cardiac Care Exercise Specialist,** Yale–New Haven Hospital, New Haven, CT 2000–Present

Assess post-cardiac surgery patients, develop and implement exercise programs, and provide strong educational component to build patients' knowledge and motivation. Deliver exercise therapy and perform patient care functions; monitor and document pre- and post-activity vital signs, cardiac rhythm, venous oxygen saturation.

Work collaboratively with health-care team, patients, and families for optimum patient outcomes.

- Played a key role in planning and developing **new educational video and print materials** to educate patients on home care procedures.
- Participate in development and delivery of **monthly educational forum for visiting physicians, surgeons, anesthesiologists, and nurses,** demonstrating innovative OPCAB procedure. (Yale–New Haven Hospital was chosen as a "Center of Excellence" by manufacturer for excellent patient results through OPCAB use.) Role in presentation is to explain and illustrate how we incorporate education, motivation, and persuasion to "sell" cardiac rehab to patients.
- Successful in **persuading and influencing** patients to make life changes for health and longevity.

SALES **Sales Representative,** Keep In Touch, West Haven, CT Part time, 2001–Present

Sell pagers and telephones to retail customers for both business and personal use. Provide sales support and resolve customer problems and questions.

- **Met or exceeded sales quotas every month** beginning with first month of employment:

Feb	Mar	Apr	May	Jun	Jul	Aug	Sep	Oct	Nov	Dec	Jan
140%	129%	115%	122%	116%	100%	118%	123%	118%	115%	106%	108%

- Maintain above-average sales and customer satisfaction through **consultative sales approach** to learn customer needs and deliver the best communication solution.

Education

Bachelor of Arts in Exercise Science / Minor in Health Promotion 2000
Quinnipiac College, Hamden, CT

INTERNSHIPS
- **Cardiac Rehabilitation,** Yale–New Haven Hospital: Learned practical application of exercise physiology for cardiac rehabilitation patients. Offered full-time position on completion of internship.
- **Corporate Fitness,** University Wellness Center
- **Health Promotion,** New Haven County Health Department

LEADERSHIP Elected to leadership positions within Kappa Sigma Sorority.

Certifications

- Advanced Cardiac Life Support (Yale–New Haven Hospital)
- Community CPR and First Aid (American Red Cross)
- Certified Instructor: Cooper/Clayton Smoking Cessation Program (American Cancer Society)

Chris is a medical exercise specialist who wants to transition to medical or pharmaceutical sales. Notice how the objective is crystal-clear and relevant qualifications and achievements are appropriately highlighted.

Alex Martinez

6525 45th Avenue SW
Seattle, WA 98136

amartinez1212@msn.com

206-453-0904 Home
206-704-2240 Mobile

SALES / MANAGEMENT

MBA (Marketing) graduate with diverse project and professional experience, an exceptional work ethic, and the drive and dedication to achieve aggressive goals. Track record of finding solutions to varied challenges and quickly succeeding in new assignments. Specific expertise within sports marketing and sales; demonstrated motivational and leadership skills. **Consistent top performer eager for new challenges.**

EDUCATION

MBA Marketing, 2003   UNIVERSITY OF WASHINGTON, Seattle, WA

► **Team Projects:** Collaborated with diverse, multicultural teammates on key projects requiring extensive coordination, multi-step action plans, and conformance with strict deadlines.
  - **Sports marketing:** Performed market research to identify ways for Nike to reach target market. Recommended use of role models and celebrities; identified influential trends. **Marketing Research Award (#1 of 6 teams).**
  - **Product development:** Researched, developed, and produced training device, "The Batboy," to help young baseball players develop core skills. **Product Innovation Technical Merit Award (#1 of 10 teams).**
  - **Entertainment industry:** Developed comprehensive sales campaign for Loews Cinemas.
  - **Packaging:** Collaborated with professionals from client company (Microsoft) to develop a solution to a packaging dilemma. Recommended new packaging and new assembly process that delivered quantifiable cost and time savings; presented recommendations to senior executives.

► **Graduate Assistant:** Management Department (1999–2001)

BS Business Administration, 1999   UNIVERSITY OF ILLINOIS, Champaign-Urbana, IL
  - **"Best Business Plan" (Entrepreneurship Class),** judged by professors and panel of investors.
  - Nominated to Beta Gamma Sigma — award honoring achievement in the study of business.
  - Nominated to Phi Kappa Phi — award recognizing excellence in all academic disciplines.
  - Starting pitcher (2 years), NCAA Division I baseball team.
  - Chancellor's Award for academic and on-field performance.

AS, 1997   DE MOINES COMMUNITY COLLEGE, Des Moines, IA
  - *Wall Street Journal* Student Achievement Award
  - 1997 NJCAA Division II championship team, Division II All-American, and Academic All-American.

EXPERIENCE

Sports Information Director / Head Baseball Coach, 2001–2002   INDIAN SPRINGS COLLEGE, Dubuque, IA
Managed athletic, administrative, and marketing functions for NCAA Division III baseball team; concurrently, served as sports information director for all 15 sports at the college.

► **Marketing / Sales:** Initiated successful drive for new baseball uniforms, raising $15,000 in sponsor funds. Used creative recruiting approaches to attract high-potential recruits. Built rapport and relationships with parents and local coaches as well as prospective players.

► **Leadership:** Despite loss of key (graduating) talent, maintained previous year's record and drove impressive improvements in key statistical areas (home runs, triples, RBIs, runs, slugging percentage, stolen bases); finished 4th among 8 teams in conference.

► **Media / Presentations:** Appeared weekly on college radio program, giving sports updates and game analyses. Provided color commentary for radio broadcasts of college basketball and football games. Served as athletic spokesperson for the college and developed excellent relationships with local media.

Professional Baseball Player Cincinnati Reds Organization—Charleston AlleyCats, Charleston, WV, 1999–2000

Alex is a recent MBA graduate who had a brief prior career as a college athletics coach. His recent educational experience and projects are emphasized because they are very relevant to his goal of a career in sales. His prior sports experience is also included with some detail because he is interested in a position in the sports-marketing field.

DARRYL T. POSTON

4525 Carmel Court, Indianapolis, IN 46210
Home 317-459-6669 ▪ Mobile 317-204-8040

TOP-PERFORMING SALES & MANAGEMENT PROFESSIONAL————————————

▪ **EXPERT CLOSING SKILLS**

Sales leader able to "hit the ground running" in challenging new environments. Highly skilled in relationship-building, customer communication, and all facets of the sales process; B2B and B2C sales experience.

Offer added value in the form of management and marketing experience, with a record of successful turnaround leadership and ability to motivate teams to improve performance and achieve results. Energized by new challenges; dedicated to building product knowledge, identifying product benefits, and finding solutions to customer problems. Excellent network of business and personal contacts in the Indianapolis area.

EXPERIENCE AND ACHIEVEMENTS————————————————————

ELITE AUTOS, Indianapolis, IN   2002–Present
Indianapolis' largest dealer of prestige vehicles—Mercedes-Benz, Jaguar, Land Rover, Volvo; recognized for exceptional customer service.

▪ **SALES CLOSER (FINANCIAL SERVICES MANAGER),** 2003–Present

Exceeded every monthly goal in sales of enhanced services and maintained closing rate of approximately 70%. As sales closer, finalize deals for purchase of new vehicles with average price of $42,000. Enhance dealership's revenue and profit margin by selling additional services— financing, leasing, extended warranties, life insurance, and accident insurance.

  ☑ Achieved consistently excellent sales performance—e.g., in April 2003, personally delivered 97% of entire dealership sales goal for enhanced services and generated more than double the revenue of dealership's other sales closer.

▪ **SALES CONSULTANT,** 2002–2003

Rapidly learned new products and new B2C sales strategies; surpassed all sales goals and earned recognition as a Mercedes-Benz Star Achiever. Managed existing account base and developed new customers for Land Rover and Mercedes-Benz vehicles.

  ☑ Consistently achieved 100% of monthly goal for number of vehicles sold.
  ☑ Attained 99.1% client-satisfaction rate for 3 straight months prior to promotion.
  ☑ Built clientele through extensive personal networking, cold-calling, and community visibility.
  ☑ Managed and maintained base of over 600 clients through frequent (every 90 days) contact.
  ☑ Completed extensive in-house sales training and Mercedes-Benz product training.

VENUE PARTNERS, Indianapolis, IN   1998–2001
Business conglomerate involved in entertainment/hospitality, advertising, and commercial real estate.

▪ **GENERAL MANAGER**

Reversed unprofitable operation, generated significant new business, and efficiently managed multiple operations. Originally recruited to manage night-shift operations; within 3 weeks, promoted to full management responsibility for restaurant/nightclub and within 4 months assumed additional managerial responsibility for full-service restaurant, outdoor-advertising business, and commercial real-estate business. Successfully performed multifaceted role in fast-paced, demanding environment. Improved operational performance of all 3 businesses.

Darryl began his career in restaurant/nightclub sales, successfully transitioned to auto sales, and now wants to make another move to sales of telecommunications services to businesses. Notice how even in his earlier, non-sales positions, his sales-related achievements are

(continues)

- **GENERAL MANAGER,** VENUE PARTNERS, continued

Restaurants: Managed hiring and training, scheduling, payroll and accounting, vendor negotiations, quality customer service, and facility maintenance; supervised 30+ staff.

☑ Turned $30K–$40K monthly loss to break-even operation within 2 years through focused attention to operational improvements, sales and marketing initiatives, and image upgrade.

☑ Transformed restaurant image to draw younger clientele with larger spending habits.

☑ In a cutthroat, competitive market, maintained share of holiday-party business through extensive marketing and networking with influential groups.

☑ Improved caliber of employees by creating a team environment and weeding out poor performers. Carefully documented all employee interactions to support firing decisions.

Commercial Real Estate: Handled all facets of advertising, sales, lease negotiation, and client presentations. Served as primary point of contact for all tenant questions and issues.

☑ Doubled occupancy rates (from 40% to 80%) through effective sales presentations that clearly communicated property benefits.

☑ Gained competitive advantage through a policy of prompt response and proactive problem solving.

Outdoor Advertising: Directed sales and customer relationship management; managed construction projects and maintenance; ensured compliance with city and state ordinances and licensing requirements.

☑ Achieved and maintained 100% rental rate, improving from 70%.

☑ Conceived innovative account-grouping approach and successfully marketed to advertising agencies as a premier client service.

EDUCATION

INDIANA UNIVERSITY, Bloomington, IN

☑ Bachelor of Science in Business Administration, 1998

COMMUNITY LEADERSHIP

INDY DOWNTOWNERS, Indianapolis, IN

☑ Member, 1998–Present

☑ Membership Chair, 2000–2001: Led the most successful membership drive in organization's history, adding 73 new members—more than double previous record of 35.

☑ President, 2001–2002: Refocused organizational activities toward community benefits (rather than purely social events); increased attendance by 20% on average and raised more than $10K to benefit Library Read-a-Thon, Special Olympics, and Heart Mini-Marathon.

(continued)

noted; and wherever possible, he provides evidence of his success in the form of hard numbers and percentages. Even his community experience is included to show that he can sell, persuade, and lead.

Trisha Benedict

1109 Corry Drive, Fresno, CA 93712
209-409-7399 ◆ tbenedict@aol.com

Goal	Sales or Customer Relationship-Management
Qualifications	◆ Ten years' experience in sales and customer services positions, with a track record of building strong customer relationships and contributing to business goals.
	◆ Outgoing personality and ability to build rapport with diverse people.
	◆ Genuine commitment to customer well-being and ability to sell solutions to customer problems.
	◆ Personal traits that include high energy level, dependability, strong work ethic, and integrity.
Experience	
2002–2003	**Sales / Makeup Artist: Estée Lauder Cosmetics**
	◆ Traveled to various department stores in Fresno area, performing customer makeovers and selling cosmetics.
	◆ Contributed to success of large-scale makeover events that delivered high sales volume.
1998–2002	**Sales / Service: Renewal Hair Replacement Systems**
1994–1998	**Sales / Service: Men's Club Hair Replacement Systems**
	◆ Promoted services and assisted clients in selecting services to meet their specific needs; also provided licensed cosmetology services for full range of hair-replacement services.
	◆ Worked one-on-one with clients, building ongoing relationships and upselling appropriate services to maintain sales volume.
	◆ Regularly earned sales commissions and bonuses based on excellent sales results.
	◆ Contributed to business growth that led to successful sale of Men's Club to a national company, Renewal; kept on staff to continue sales and service in new organization.
1990–1994	**Cosmetologist: Hair Salons in Greater Fresno**
Education	
1990	**Cosmetology License**
	California College of Hair Design: Sacramento, California

In this resume, you can see how Trisha presented her customer-service and cosmetology experience with a sales slant. Because she is pursuing a full-time sales position with a hair-products or cosmetics company, her experience is highly relevant even though most of it has not been in direct-sales roles.

James Williams

1094 Bridge Street, Columbus, OH 43228
604-243-0931 • jameswill@earthlink.net

Goal: Technical Sales / Sales Engineer

Engineering professional with broad knowledge and proven skills that point to success in sales:

- **Technical expertise:** Ten years' experience in advanced engineering research and project management; broad knowledge of mechanical, aerospace, civil, and environmental engineering.
- **Communication skills and business knowledge:** Ability to convey technical concepts; experience delivering corporate presentations; understanding of business demands that drive buying decisions.
- **Problem-solving and customer satisfaction skills:** Track record of devising innovative solutions to diverse problems and working successfully with academic and corporate staff.
- **Eagerness to tackle new challenges:** Demonstrated ability to manage multiple projects and thrive in demanding environments. Record of leadership, strong work ethic, and commitment to excel.

Experience and Achievements

RESEARCH ASSOCIATE: Aerospace Department, The Ohio State University   1993–2003

As an integral part of the engineering research team, provided hands-on project management assistance to Ph.D. engineering students. Assessed project feasibility, gathered and analyzed data, created and oversaw project protocols to bring engineering concepts to fruition. Interacted with and reported to business sponsors interested in project commercialization.

Consistently met deadlines and delivered project components on or ahead of schedule while overseeing multiple concurrent projects.

- Recognized for ability to assess practicality of project concepts and to lead project team in developing outlines and protocols for start-to-finish process management.
- Recommended combining undergraduate aerospace and mechanical engineering labs to avoid duplication of experimentation and therefore deliver ongoing cost savings to both departments.
- Took the lead in investigating outsource capabilities, performing feasibility and cost comparisons, and choosing outside services when time and cost savings could be achieved.
- Reduced departmental expense for its high-pressure air system by calculating cost-per-pound and creating structure and system to charge other departments appropriately for use of this equipment.
- Maintained excellent relationships with corporate sponsors from companies such as General Electric, Pratt & Whitney, Rolls Royce, and Procter and Gamble. Delivered progress reports and effectively communicated complex engineering/research concepts and findings.
- Participated in diverse mechanical, biomechanical, civil, and environmental engineering projects; gained broad knowledge of combustors, gas turbines, wind tunnels, instrumentation, measuring devices, thermocouples, data acquisition equipment, and pressure devices.

Education

Bachelor of Science in Mechanical Engineering (BSME), 1990   The Ohio State University

Additional Qualifications

- Keenly interested in both design and hands-on application of design principles. Designed and personally built three homes; designed and constructed an airplane; designed and built automobiles.
- Computer skills include Windows-based business software, Turtle programming, Pascal, AutoCAD.

Professional Affiliation

Member, Society of Manufacturing Engineers

This resume makes the case for James' transition from engineering research to technical sales. A good many technical details are included because his engineering knowledge will be important to his next employer. Also included are indicators of his business savvy and communications skills.

ELISABETH KOHL

781-243-0094 25 Cranberry Court, Needham, MA 02492 ekohl@verizon.net

SALES & MARKETING
Consultative Sales — Account Management — Customer Relationship-Building

- **Proven Sales Talents:** Consistent top performer in sales of services and intangibles. Demonstrated expertise in the sales cycle from cold-calling and qualifying through needs assessment, presentation, and closing.

- **Sales Training Expertise:** Able to teach fundamental sales skills, sharpen closing abilities, and mentor and develop sales teams to top performance.

- **Persuasive Communication:** Successful in overcoming objections, presenting / selling intangibles, developing business alliances, and maintaining excellent customer relationships.

EXPERIENCE

Center Director   MatchMates, Boston, MA — 2001–Present

- Perform multifaceted sales / management / training role for 900-member Boston office of one of the nation's largest private dating clubs.
  — Quickly increased revenues and leaped from last to **#2** of 6 branches.
- Develop monthly sales projections, sales strategies, and action plans.
  — Consistently meet monthly sales goals and deliver more than **$1 million** in annual revenue.
- Hire, train, and develop new employees; manage staff of 5. Supervise sales presentations and close sales for inexperienced sales reps.
  — Trained both new and experienced sales staff in fundamental sales skills such as qualifying and screening prospects, overcoming objections, and closing the sale.
  — **All** sales staff now meet goal of closing **50%** of sales, with best reps achieving close to **80%** closure rate.
  — Personally close **80+%** of sales.
- Create marketing ideas that increase productivity and profitability.
  — Initiated diverse social events that have become a key selling point of our service.
  — Initiated radio-station partnership and event co-sponsorship to boost visibility among prime demographic target.
- Qualify prospective members through 90-minute pre-screening interviews.
  — Retained **50%** of members in first renewal opportunity for 2-year-old office.

Corporate Travel Agent   Far & Away Travel, Needham, MA — 1990–1994

- Arranged and sold travel services to both corporate and leisure travelers.
- Trained new employees with a focus on consultative sales and cross-selling.

EDUCATION / CERTIFICATION / COMPUTER SKILLS

- Bunker Hill Community College
  — Associate of Science degree, 1988
- Travel Trainers, Inc., Lawrence, MA
  — Certified Travel Consultant (CTC), 1990
- Proficient in Windows-based business software including Microsoft Word, Excel, and Publisher.

Although most of Elisabeth's job consisted of management responsibilities, she did have some direct-sales activities and was instrumental in closing sales for her staff. To support her decision to transition to a pure sales career, her resume highlights those sales activities and achievements while downplaying the management role.

Kara Fitzhugh

11209 Cherry Tree Drive, Dunwoody, GA 30338

Home (770) 234-0432 • Office (440) 881-9704 • Email karafitzhugh@hotmail.com

Goal   **Sales — Sales Support Team Leadership — Manufacturing Environment**

Summary
- Successful track record in sales of technical services—national and international environments.
- Proven capabilities in staff training, mentoring, development, and motivation.
- Ability to create persuasive sales presentations for internal and external customers.
- Measurable improvements in service delivery time, customer satisfaction, results tracking, and other performance criteria.

Professional Experience

SOUTHERN PAPER TECHNOLOGY, Atlanta, Georgia, 1990–Present
$50 million division of German-owned machinery manufacturer for the paper-making industry

Manager, Customer Service, 2000–Present

Selected to lead newly formed department consolidating Technical Services and Spare Parts operations following corporate merger. Managed growth of department from 8 people in 2000 to 16 currently. Interact with corporate HQ in Germany, parts facilities in Austria and Brazil, and customers throughout U.S., Mexico, and Canada; travel to corporate and customer facilities as needed.

Oversee the activities of Field Technical Service Engineers, Commissioning Engineers, and Spare Parts team; manage $5.5 million sales budget. Additionally, provide direct service to key accounts, resolving issues and problems in a high-pressure service environment for customers whose productivity depends on machine reliability.

- Increased sale of services 25% while maintaining budgeted percentage of direct hours and profit margins.
- Managed the department as a revenue-generator while maintaining consistently positive customer relations.
- Created a tracking system to identify key customer concerns and monitor average response times. Used data as an analytical tool for department decision-making. Successfully and continually reduced average response times.
- Developed departmental procedures and guidelines for customer response; trained staff in service delivery to ensure consistent and customer-focused service.
- By swiftly addressing customer issues, slashed active customer concerns by 50%.
- Supported growth and development of individual staff members through ongoing training, incentive programs, and opportunities for decision-making and autonomy.
- Participated on company-wide task force that developed a new national sales program.

Manager, Sales Administration, 1997–2000

Assumed management of Spare Parts department while retaining all prior Sales Supervisor responsibilities. Directed 8-member staff and managed $3 million spare parts budget.

- Increased profit margins 25% while growing spare parts business 20%.
- Reduced order entry time and customer confirmation time by 50%.
- Created spare-parts database that provided immediate access to pricing and usage information for all key accounts and was easily updated to reflect current activity.

After more than a decade in diverse roles (most of them sales related) for a machinery manufacturer, Kara wanted to make a move. Her ideal next position was in direct sales to manufacturing companies like hers, but she would also consider a management position in a sales-support organization. This resume clearly spells out both her manufacturing expertise and her ability to be successful in multiple facets of sales.

Sales Supervisor, 1994–1997

Led 4-person team in the development of sales/service proposals for projects ranging from $500K to $50 million. Interacted extensively with customers and field sales team on project specifications.

Senior Sales Correspondent, 1993–1994
Sales Correspondent, 1991–1993

Provided inside sales support to field sales team. Gathered specifications and wrote proposals. Accompanied sales team on customer visits to provide proposal and sales support expertise.

Estimator, 1990–1991

Generated detailed cost estimates for parts, machine components, and entire machine purchase and installation.

Education and Professional Development

EMORY UNIVERSITY, Atlanta, Georgia

- Bachelor of Science in Business Administration

IN-HOUSE COURSES

- Team Building — completed training and participated on corporate team-building task force
- Conducting Business Overseas

DALE CARNEGIE

- 12-week Communications program

Computer Skills

Proficient in Microsoft Word, Excel, and PowerPoint — FileMaker Pro database — BPCS operating system — AS400 and PC computer systems

DANIEL C. TAN

2345 Bluejay Terrace
Providence, RI 02910

cdtan@verizon.net

401-791-0904 Home
401-400-6301 Mobile

GOAL	**Sales of Public Safety Technology Products/Services to Police, Fire & Emergency Services Operations**
QUALIFICATIONS	■ High level of credibility and rapport with law enforcement, fire/safety, and municipal government representatives, gained during 25 years in law enforcement.
	■ Twelve years' experience specifying, designing, installing, upgrading, maintaining, and training users on customized police management information systems.
	■ Keen ability to explain complex technical information to non-technical audiences.

PROFESSIONAL EXPERIENCE

PROVIDENCE POLICE DEPARTMENT, Providence, RI   1978–Present

COORDINATOR: POLICE MANAGEMENT INFORMATION SYSTEMS, 1991–Present   Rank: Sergeant

Primary coordinator for all IS systems and services for department that has been a technology leader and innovator. Manage specifications, system design, implementation, and operations for 18 custom applications affecting every facet of police operations. Manage technology projects start-to-finish; direct the programming teams (both consultants and employees); oversee more than $1 million in technology investment annually.

Components	Database	Permits	Traffic Citation	Parking Citation
	Pawn Shop	Broadcast	Personnel	CAD
	MIS			

Other Systems	Radio system (Motorola Type II)	Mobile Display Terminals

Highlights	■ Chosen for position to spearhead the department's conversion to custom MIS system modeled on the FBI's National Incident Base Reporting System (NIBRS). Working with consultant contractors, efficiently managed massive department changeover.
	■ Attained measurable improvements in department's ability to perform its core functions: Reduced turnaround time from incident occurrence to initiation of police investigation from 15 days to 25 minutes; solved previously unsolvable crimes due to availability of information; increased officers' efficiency by reducing time required for report-taking.
	■ Led successful culture shift, overcoming traditionalism and resistance to change by "selling" benefits and advantages of new system. Able to communicate effectively with individuals at all levels of the department through established credibility and trust.
	■ As liaison with senior police and city officials, regularly provided information that aided in policy development, decision-making, scheduling, and other management activities.
	■ Managed $5 million project to completely overhaul the radio system used for all public safety activities in the city of Providence. Assessed needs, specified equipment, oversaw channel programming, and managed smooth conversion.
	■ Instrumental in establishing police department program to train officers in mediation and creating system for referring appropriate cases to city mediation center.
	■ Named "Providence Police Office of the Year" 1992 — first officer chosen for ongoing activities rather than high-profile heroism.

LAW ENFORCEMENT OFFICER, 1975–1998

EDUCATION	■ Bachelor of Science in Criminal Justice, 1991: Anna Maria College, Paxton, MA
	■ Police Officer Training, 1975: Providence Police Officer Academy

COMMUNITY	■ **Mediator,** Providence Mediation Center, 1995–Present — First police officer to become a mediator with this city agency. **Advisory Board Chairman,** 1999–2001.

Daniel used this resume to transition from a career as a police officer into sales. He had been in charge of technology systems for the police department. This expertise, combined with his deep knowledge of law-enforcement and public-safety operations, made him an attractive candidate to companies that sell systems to these organizations.

Continue Communicating in Your Cover Letters

Introduce your resume with a cover letter that highlights your interest in sales and your strongest qualifications for the position you're seeking. If you have no experience in sales, you can't claim that as a primary qualification—but you can talk about communication skills, knowledge of the company's products or customers, planning and organizational skills, and other characteristics that you know are important.

Note how the following two cover letters clearly communicate knowledge of what it takes to be successful in sales—and how the candidate has shown those skills and traits.

Lee S. Hightower

45 Shoreline Drive, East Haven, CT 06512 • (860) 877-3211 • leehigh@snet.net

May 15, 2003

Hiram T. Ross
VP Sales & Marketing
Worldwide Widgets
259 Industrial Parkway
Orange, CT 06477

Dear Mr. Ross:

You may recall our conversation last month about sales opportunities with Worldwide Widgets. One of the characteristics of a successful sales professional is persistence... and I don't intend to give up trying until I am successful in joining one of the best sales teams in the business and one of the best organizations in town!

When you are considering candidates for your next sales opening, please keep in mind these core capabilities and expertise relevant to your needs:

- ☑ Deep understanding of the widget industry and expert knowledge of your suppliers, customers, and competitors through my 10-year career with Acme Widgets.

- ☑ Exceptional relationship-building skills—and the ability to professionally leverage relationships for mutual benefit.

- ☑ High energy level, strong work ethic, and drive to reach ever-expanding goals.

I am confident I will quickly become a top performer for your organization. Can we set up a meeting to discuss this idea? I have enclosed my resume for your further consideration and will follow up with a phone call early next week.

Thank you.

Sincerely,

Lee S. Hightower

enclosure

This letter starts off with a bang—right up front it introduces traits that are important for success in sales. The traits are supported by core knowledge and qualifications highlighted in the three bullet points. Note the polite yet assertive close.

Subject: Sales Representative—Western Region—Job Posting #549-S-W

I am very interested in bringing my experience and abilities to an innovative industry leader and would like to discuss the value I offer in a sales role with Medical Marvels.

With education and experience in healthcare combined with a successful background in sales, I offer qualities that closely match your needs:

== Three years' experience in direct patient care in a hospital environment... knowledge of hospital operations and ability to interact effectively with diverse healthcare professionals.

== Twelve months of exceeding all quotas in a fast-paced sales environment.

== Excellent presentation skills... evidenced through monthly presentations to cardiologists and other healthcare professionals and selection for an educational video on post-cardiac care.

== Strong communication skills and ability to persuade and influence customers, patients, and other healthcare professionals.

The position with Medical Marvels is exciting, and I would welcome the opportunity to explore how I can contribute to your company's continued growth and success.

Sincerely,

Chris Canyon

=================
My resume is attached as a Word document, as specified in your posting.

Formatted as an e-mail message, this letter will be accompanied by an attached resume file. The subject line clearly identifies the reason for the e-mail. The paragraphs are short and punchy for easy on-screen reading. Again, bullet points are used to identify core qualifications.

Selling Yourself Through Networking

Networking is the most important strategy you can pursue when searching for a new job. It's particularly effective and essential when you're making a career shift. It's also a skill you can use every day of your business life to be more successful as well as make a greater contribution to your company's goals.

The good news is that people who are good at sales are often naturally good at networking. Networking simply means talking to people, building relationships, and asking for information, referrals, guidance, suggestions, and ideas. Just as importantly, meaningful networking involves giving as well as getting. So the more you do to give to your network of friends, colleagues, and relatives, the more you'll get back and the deeper your resources will be when you have a specific need.

Here's a simple seven-step process you can follow for effective networking in your current job search and well beyond.

1. **Define what you want from your network.** Be specific about what you need: The name of a top salesperson at a particular company? Suggestions for companies that might make use of your expertise in a sales role? Review of your resume? Referral to a hiring manager? Information on the particular industry or company you're targeting? People will be glad to help you as long as they know how, provided that you don't ask them for something they can't give you (such as a job).

2. **Make a list of your network.** "Your network" is, quite simply, everyone you know, and it will grow as people you know refer you to people they know. Categorize your list into "A," "B," and "C" contacts, based on your initial impression of how helpful they can be in your search. "A" contacts include anyone in sales; anyone who works at a company or in an industry you're targeting; any executive of any company in your geographic area—in short, anyone who might be able to give you directly relevant information, leads, or referrals. "B" contacts are those on

the periphery of your targets, whereas "C" contacts would be everyone else. Of course, you can never tell who people know, and a "C" contact might be related in some way to one of your top targets, so don't neglect the "C" list entirely!

3. **Create a systematic plan for contacting everyone on your list.** Be diligent and persistent in making those calls and trying to set up in-person meetings. Just as you would in a sales job, set specific goals for the number of calls you'll make every day and the number of appointments per week you'll schedule. Don't give up until you've reached your goals.

4. **Be prepared to tell your contacts what you're looking for,** how they can help you, why you've decided on a sales career, and—importantly—what you've done so far. Your contacts will be motivated to help you if they see you're serious and have done the necessary groundwork.

5. **Follow up on every lead,** suggestion, and referral your contacts give you.

6. **Periodically get back in touch with your contacts.** Give them a status report, tell them the results of their previous suggestions, and ask for help in a new, specific area.

7. **When you've finally landed your new job, send a thank-you note and update to every one of your sources.** Offer to help them in any way you can. And keep your contacts alive—you'll find them an invaluable advantage in your new career.

Selling Yourself in Interviews

Once your networking efforts, combined with your resume and cover letter, start to generate interviews for you, you'll want to be sure you communicate effectively when you meet with potential employers. Prepare yourself to answer this all-important question, whether it be spoken or unspoken: "Why should I hire you?"

Study the strategies in the following sections as you prepare to sell yourself in the interview process.

Understand Your Value to the Company

As we've discussed earlier in this chapter, companies want to hire people who can solve problems for them. You'll increase your chances of getting a job offer if you clearly show that you understand the company's problems and have ideas for solutions. Be sure you've done your homework to learn all you can about the company, its customers, its markets, its competitors, its growth opportunities, and its strategic plans. Then refer to those when you answer the interviewer's questions. Here's an example of how to do this:

Tell me about yourself.

Well, I come to sales from a rather unusual background! After five years as a C++ and Java programmer with Plaintech Solutions, I wanted more customer interaction and the opportunity to see how my programs were being used in daily business operations. So I asked for and was given the opportunity to transfer to the help desk, where for a year I did nothing but answer customers' questions and help them be more productive with the software. Last year I was promoted to manage that operation, and while I've enjoyed the challenge I've also discovered that direct interaction with customers is my real passion and strength. When your company's problems with customer satisfaction became well known through the press last month, I was excited to read about your plan to beef up your technical sales staff. I think I'd be a great fit for your expanded sales force. I have strong technical skills, a great customer-service approach, and a real passion for making software work better. That's why I'm here today—to see what the opportunities are in your sales organization and how I can add value to your new business direction.

Be Prepared to Elaborate on Why You Want a Career in Sales

But don't make it all about yourself. You'll earn points in your favor if you mention that you can help the company increase its sales, better serve its customers, capture new business, and other benefits of an effective sales force. Here's an example:

> *I hope you can tell that I've given a lot of thought to my next position. Working on fund drives for the March of Dimes and United Way taught me that I love the personal interaction and persuasion that are involved in sales, and when I saw how my efforts produced great results, it was really gratifying. My experience at Consolidated Companies gives me a lot of knowledge about your suppliers and competitors, and I'm confident I can convert that to benefits for your company and its customers. I really thrive on new challenges and would love to set sales records for your company.*

Practice Telling Your "Success Stories" in a Way That's Meaningful and Understandable

When you use a story to back up a "theoretical" answer ("Here's how I'd handle that kind of challenge…and here's how I did something like it recently"), you do a great job of making that theory a concrete fact. So prepare by rehearsing various success stories in the "CAR" (Challenge—Actions—Result) format. This format tells a story logically, for easy understanding, and is a wonderful way to showcase both your problem-solving style and the results you were able to get. Here's an example:

> *How would I deal with a demanding boss? I think being really clear about expectations is the best approach. It prevents misunderstandings and makes sure my boss and I are on the same page. At Acme Fittings, I worked for a manager who was considered the most demanding in the company. In fact, she had a hard time keeping her staff positions*

filled. What I did to clarify expectations was schedule a brief meeting with her every Friday morning to review what I had done for the week and where I was going to focus my attention the next week. I followed up that meeting with a memo that put everything in writing and gave her the chance to make any changes before the new week started. As a result, she knew my progress and my intentions at all times, and she learned that she could trust me to do what we had agreed. I ended up working for her for three years and found her to be a great manager who really wanted me to succeed.

Be Prepared for the "But You Have No Experience" Statement

If you're new to sales, you might feel like the opportunity's dead when the interview brings up this point. But don't despair! Often the interviewer simply wants to remove what might be an obstacle to hiring you. If you can explain that you have studied what it takes to be successful, and that you have the traits and abilities you think are most important, you'll show the interviewer that you understand the challenges, are willing to work to succeed, and have the fundamental abilities to do the job. For example:

You're right, I don't have any direct sales experience. But in all of my activities, no matter what my formal job, I've always played a sales role. For instance, when I was Treasurer of Delta Delta Delta, I volunteered to head up the recruiting committee that increased our membership for the first time in 12 years. At Superfood, I drummed up so much support for our volunteer programs, we were named 'Volunteer of the Year' by the United Way. And as a member of the Leadership Initiative, I not only planned campus-improvement programs, I had to use sales strategies to get funding, volunteers, and support from the administration. I've always used sales skills to accomplish the things that I think are important, and now I'd like to use them full time in my career.

Be Enthusiastic

Employers want to hire people who are excited about the opportunity and the company—people who *want* to work for them. Don't be afraid to show your enthusiasm and eagerness to get started.

> *This opportunity sounds like a great fit for me! You mentioned the challenges of entering this new market. I see them more as opportunities to have a real impact on company sales, and I'm eager to get started!*

Ask for the Job!

It is extremely important at the end of the interview to ask for the job. This is the same thing as closing a sale. Here, you are selling yourself. Sales managers and human resource personnel expect sales candidates to ask for the job. There are several ways to do this.

Start with an open-ended question: "How do you feel my traits and skills match this exciting opportunity?" Notice that this question requires a detailed answer as opposed to "yes" or "no." This question will help you uncover any concerns the interviewer might have about your qualifications.

If the answer is positive, show that you really want the job. "I am pleased to hear that because I would like to have this position. When can I start?" Or in a situation where you are being interviewed by several people at the company, you might say "Can I count on your support when you review my qualifications with your colleagues?" Most interviewers will smile at these questions and give you a vague answer. However, they know you asked for the job. That's what is important.

If the answer to the first question seems awkward or negative, you should try to find out what is behind this behavior. You might then say "Is there some additional information I could provide to you about my qualifications?" Or you could conclude with, "I can imagine that you are concerned with my lack of actual sales experience; however, as I explained earlier, I have demonstrated the important traits and skills necessary to succeed. I would really like this exciting position. What is the next step in the interviewing process?"

Wrap-up and To Do

Follow the steps outlined in this chapter to define and continually refine your targets, put together your marketing materials (resume and cover letters), use your network to help you get information and interviews, and sell yourself as the solution to an employer's problems.

Use the worksheets on the next few pages as a resource and guideline.

One of the most beneficial things you can do is build your network; it will help you make connections and smooth your path in all kinds of circumstances that go well beyond your current career transition. The best way to have a great network is to be a sought-after network contact and valuable resource for others—someone people turn to when they have a problem, question, or need. Dedicate yourself to creating and nurturing this network not for your immediate benefit but instead as a rewarding, satisfying, lifelong way to connect with people.

Finally, practice, practice, and practice more. Answer some of the questions in the preceding section in front of the mirror or with a friend or spouse. Your ability to articulate answers to difficult questions will show that you can think on your feet and demonstrates confidence. Practicing your networking "speech" is important, too.

My Target Lists

Industries	Qualifications Required	Contacts/ Referrals	Notes

Companies	Qualifications Required	Contacts/ Referrals	Notes

Resume and Cover Letter Worksheet

Objective _____

Summary Of Qualifications

My strongest selling points:

_____

_____

_____

_____

_____

_____

Success stories to illustrate my strongest selling points:

_____

_____

_____

_____

_____

_____

_____

_____

_____

_____

_____

_____

_____

_____

Chronological Work Experience

Most Recent Position

Company name, city, state _____

Dates of employment _____

Job title _____

Activities related to sales goal _____

_____

_____

_____

_____

_____

_____

_____

Achievements (including numbers and other quantifiable measurements of success)

_____

_____

_____

_____

_____

Previous Position

Company name, city, state _____

Dates of employment _____

Job title _____

(continues)

147

(continued)

Activities related to sales goal _____

_____

_____

_____

_____

Achievements (including numbers and other quantifiable measurements of success)

_____

_____

_____

_____

Previous Position

Company name, city, state _____

Dates of employment _____

_____

Job title _____

_____

Activities related to sales goal _____

_____

_____

_____

Achievements (including numbers and other quantifiable measurements of success)

_____

_____

_____

_____

Previous Position

Company name, city, state _____

Dates of employment _____

Job title _____

Activities related to sales goal _____

_____

_____

_____

Achievements (including numbers and other quantifiable measurements of success)

_____

_____

_____

_____

Additional Qualifications

Skills, knowledge, activities, and achievements related to sales goal _____

_____

_____

_____

_____

_____

_____

_____

_____

_____

_____

(continues)

(continued)

Education

College, city, state _____

_____

_____

Degree _____

_____

Major/minor _____

_____

GPA/academic achievements _____

_____

Extracurricular activities and achievements related to sales goal (including success stories) _____

_____

_____

_____

_____

_____

Notes for Cover Letters

Problems or needs I've uncovered about this company or industry in my research

_____

_____

_____

Opening paragraph (why am I writing?)_____

_____

_____

_____

_____

Middle section (what will interest the reader?) _____

_____

_____

_____

_____

_____

Closing (how will I follow up?) _____

_____

_____

_____

_____

_____

_____

_____

_____

_____

CHAPTER 8 Sales Career Paths

Like most careers, sales offers opportunities for advancement—to a management position, to an expanded sales and marketing role, to executive-level sales and marketing, and even to general management and senior executive roles. But unlike a lot of fields, sales can provide continuous increases in compensation and ongoing job satisfaction even if you stay in direct sales for your entire career. That's because there is always something new in sales—new products, new technology, new customers, new competition, territory realignment, and other changes that keep salespeople on their toes. If nothing else, there are always new quotas to meet, new methods to try, and prospective customers to win over.

Whether you choose to stay in direct sales or move up, you'll want to think about where your career might lead and how you can best prepare to take on the challenges of a new role. Common career paths in sales include the following:

- Pure sales

- Sales to marketing

- Sales to sales management

- Sales or marketing management to general management

This chapter discusses the foundation of any sales career—success in your first job—and shows you how to make your way along the career path of your choosing.

Initial Success

Being successful in your first sales position is important to any career path you choose. The elements of success in sales are the following:

1. Achieving sales goals or targets

2. Gaining a clear understanding of products and/or services

3. Establishing and maintaining good relationships with customers

4. Practicing good communication with your superiors and mentors, including being willing to ask for help

5. Putting in the hours of work to accomplish steps 1 through 4

These points might seem pretty basic—and in fact, if you work diligently on each of the steps, we can just about guarantee that you will succeed! But as in any new venture, there is a learning curve. As a new sales rep, you will be given some leeway in performance if it is obvious that you are making the effort to succeed.

As we said in chapter 5, "The Art and Science of Sales," there is a methodology to sales. If it is followed with persistence, success will result. The first few months of a sales position are an important investment in your future success. You will need to work overtime, studying product information and sales-training information at night while you call on customers during the day. If you are selling a product such as cosmetics through home-based sales, this schedule might be reversed. You might be studying when possible during the day so that you can talk to people when they are at home at night.

Then you need to be organized and practice your presentations. Practice breeds confidence. People like to buy from confident salespeople. It makes them feel more secure in their purchase decision. Sitting in front of a mirror and making a presentation is a very good way to practice. Running through a presentation in your mind is no substitute for actually saying the words while you pull out product literature and/or samples. You will be surprised that what seems simple in your mind becomes an exercise of tripping on your tongue when you verbalize it. However, after a few attempts, you will "get it." You will be ready to go.

After your first few sales calls or experiences, be proactive and call your superior and/or fellow salespeople. Share your experience and get their feedback. People love to share sales stories, and you will find this sharing to be a motivating experience. You will be energized and ready to make more sales calls.

And don't be afraid to share your sales "failures" as well. You will make some mistakes that will cause you to not get a sale. That's okay—it's to be expected. You have to give yourself a chance to learn. Learning from your mistakes, then moving ahead, is all part of building your expertise in sales. Give yourself a chance to succeed.

Careers in Direct Sales

Advancing within the field of sales usually means that you get the opportunity to earn more commissions by selling higher-value products, serving a higher-level client base, or managing fewer but more lucrative accounts. There are primarily five ways to do this:

- Take a stepping-stone approach within your industry to higher-value products.

- Earn greater sales responsibility within your current company and territory (customer grouping).

- Attain higher-level sales responsibility at your company.

- Move into sales training.

- Become an independent representative.

The following sections give details on each of these career strategies.

The Stepping-Stone Approach

The opportunity to take a stepping-stone approach is available in many industries. What we mean by this is that the salesperson starts at a basic level within an industry and over a period of 10 or 20 years moves from company to company seeking greater product sophistication. Of course, more sophisticated products usually equate to higher earnings. The base salaries go up and the commission potential increases. As important, the psychic reward goes up as well. The salesperson is dealing with more exciting products and constantly learning new things. Frequently in this situation, the salesperson is staying in the same geography and even working with some of the same customers throughout all these changes.

A good example of this is the medical-products industry. You could start out as a pharmaceutical representative selling basic eye-care drugs to ophthalmologists and optometrists. The reason we say "basic" is that there are several levels of product sophistication even within the pharmaceutical industry. More than likely you would be working for a large company with very good sales training and managerial support. You would learn a lot in this first position about selling and territory management. If you excelled over a three-year period, you would become a prime candidate for a move up to entry-level surgical products such as basic surgical instruments and surgical supplies for ophthalmologists. Excel once again, and three or four years later you could advance to higher-level surgical products such as lasers or eye implants (intraocular lenses). In this example, you would have jumped from $60,000 to $90,000 to $150,000 or more in annual income over a period of 10 years. Pictorially, it looks like this:

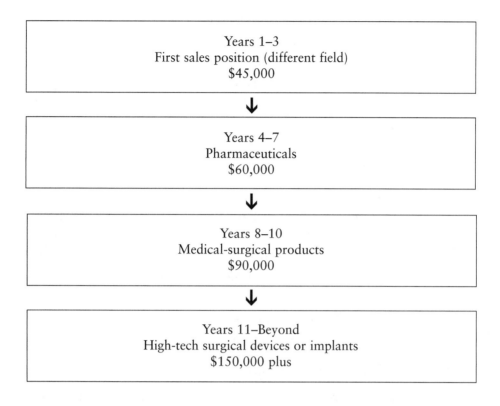

Years 1–3
First sales position (different field)
$45,000

Years 4–7
Pharmaceuticals
$60,000

Years 8–10
Medical-surgical products
$90,000

Years 11–Beyond
High-tech surgical devices or implants
$150,000 plus

Earn Greater Sales Responsibility Within Your Own Firm

Many large companies are concerned about the stepping-stone scenario described in the preceding section. They invest lots of resources in helping people become productive sales representatives. When he was VP of Sales for Mentor, a manufacturer of plastic surgery products, Ted calculated that he invested about $50,000 in each new salesperson (recruiting, interviewing, and training). Big companies such as Johnson & Johnson invest much more than this. Add to this the fact that the rep is part of a team of people who enjoy working together. Because of this, companies hate to lose a good salesperson.

To prevent the losses, they create "promotional opportunities" within the sales role. For example, someone could progress from sales representative to account manager to senior account manager. With each promotion, the salary increases and perhaps the individual gets other perks such as the eligibility to select a higher-grade company car. Senior-level salespeople might also be invited to participate in more product-development meetings. This is very satisfying. The salary is going up every few years and involvement in the company is increasing. In a company such as Johnson & Johnson, sales professionals might be able to move from one medical product division to another and have access to more sophisticated products and higher compensation.

Another way to advance within your own company is by being chosen for new areas of growth. For instance, when a company is introducing a new product, entering a new market, or launching a new sales channel, it recruits internally to fill the sales roles for this new venture.

If you are interested in these kinds of new challenges, you will increase your chances of being selected if you do the following:

- Achieve excellent sales results in your current position.
- Earn sales awards that show you can "come out of the gate" quickly and strongly.
- Build relationships throughout the company, especially with influential sales and marketing executives.
- Express interest and enthusiasm for the company's new ventures.
- Tackle new sales challenges with zest and get quick results.
- Share with your colleagues and managers your ideas and strategies for market expansion.
- Build your knowledge about new industries or markets the company might be targeting.

This sales-growth option can be very satisfying. You get rewarded for your loyalty to one company. You don't have to change sales jobs to advance in some responsibilities and to earn more money. The compensation jumps might not be as high as in the first example we gave, but the risk is a bit less. For people who want some stability in the world of sales, this can be the best path to take.

Attain Higher Level Sales Responsibility at Your Company

The third route can involve a job change or more likely is an adjunct to the second growth model. After a number of years of successful sales achievement within a company, a salesperson might be a candidate for a higher-level sales role. This role might involve more geography and higher-level customers. However, it is still primarily a sales role as opposed to a management role.

These types of premier sales positions might be referred to by titles such as *account executive, national account manager,* or *key account manager.* Sometimes these roles are so important that they are given a vice president title even though they involve little or no management of subordinates. The idea of the high-level title is to give the customer the message that the company is sending its best salesperson to work with them.

These positions involve less prospecting and cold-calling and more relationship-building with your company's major accounts. They require a very strong customer focus and dedication to solving customers' problems—in effect, the salesperson partners with the customer to find the best solutions to help both companies grow.

To be considered a strong candidate for these positions, you should do the following:

- Achieve excellent sales results in your current position.

- Earn sales awards to boost your visibility throughout the company.

- Demonstrate exceptional customer care—go "above and beyond" as a matter of course.

- Be creative in brainstorming and problem-solving solutions to your company's and your customers' problems.

- Show that you can handle a heavy travel schedule (if you are interested in moving up to represent national accounts).

- Become very knowledgeable about your company's products and how they fit into your customers' industries.

- Build excellent relationships with your customers and people within your company.

One good example of a national account position can be found in consumer products. A large consumer-products company such as Black & Decker considers Home Depot to be a very important customer. Of course, Black & Decker will have local sales reps responsible for the individual Home Depot stores. But they will also want to create a high-level relationship with the executives at Home Depot. They will need someone who can work with Home Depot on a national level. This person will be trying to convince Home Depot to carry a broader line of products. Perhaps he or she will be trying to get agreement from Home Depot to locate Black & Decker products in more prominent locations for better consumer access. Or this account manager might develop a co-marketing campaign with Home Depot. These are all high-level activities that require a sophisticated, confident, professional, and detail-oriented individual. He or she will be dealing with the executives at Home Depot who make decisions involving tens of millions of dollars in product purchases. The success this person has with Home Depot will have a major impact on the fortunes of Black & Decker. Once product promotional programs with Home Depot are agreed to, the implementation is passed down to the field sales reps.

Move into Sales Training

The fourth path for advancing within the field of sales is to become a *sales trainer*. A salesperson often continues to manage a sales territory while serving as sales trainer. You would be expected to deliver your own sales results while helping others to become more effective sales-people. Often, but not always, this role is a precursor to promotion to sales manager. To boost your chances of being chosen for a sales train-er's role, you should do the following:

- Achieve excellent sales results in your current position.

- Show that you can take on special projects or extra assignments without your sales performance suffering.

- Share your expertise in sales meetings with your manager and peers.

- Offer to help a salesperson who is having a tough time.

- Volunteer for high-visibility assignments such as learning about a new product and sharing your knowledge with the rest of the sales team.

- Show leadership in learning, trying, and sharing new sales tech-niques.

Being a sales trainer is particularly rewarding and fun. As a trainer, you get to work with a large number of people and see them grow. You will be responsible for their success and might get paid accord-ingly. The position doesn't always involve direct management of sub-ordinates, but it allows you to get a feel for working through others. You can stay in this role or move on to management.

In advancing the salespeople who worked for him, Ted always used the position of sales trainer as a step toward management. Frequently, a sales trainer would keep some sales responsibility for a smaller ter-ritory. A smaller territory or customer grouping would free up the time for the training activities. At the same time, the trainer was still directly involved in sales. Finally, the trainer could return to a 100 per-cent sales role if the training activity was not successful or enjoyable.

Become an Independent Representative

Independent representatives are essentially salespeople who are in business for themselves. Usually they choose to do this after a successful career in sales in a particular industry. Many senior sales reps who feel that they have reached a dead end with their employers decide to become independents to have more control over their lives and a higher income. An independent rep typically has several products from several different manufacturers that he sells in a restricted geography. The compensation is 100 percent commission. The rep is responsible for all of his or her own business expenses.

Who uses independent reps? For the most part, independent reps are employed by small companies that can't afford to fund a direct sales force of their own. During the initial phases of their growth, they use independent sales reps to sell their products. Then as the company gets larger, it can shift to direct sales reps (its own employees). Occasionally, in certain industries, you can find large companies that always use independent representatives. Usually, they are premier companies with ultra-high expectations of the independent reps. They also have very rigid contracts. However, the commissions they pay can be extraordinarily high.

To be successful as an independent, you must know your industry and all the customers very well. You must also be effective working on your own with no supervision and minimal support from the small companies you represent. Financially, you must be prepared to weather big swings in income. As you get started, there might be many months of low income as you take on product lines and start building sales.

Just reading the description of this sales option, you can imagine the risks it involves. What if, after you have invested one or two years creating sales for a small company, it takes the product away from you as it goes direct? What if the sales from this same company represented 30 percent of your income? Or what if the company does not succeed and goes bankrupt? It leaves you with customers who have no place to go for service. This happens all the time. For the individual who can handle these risks and has access to products from new companies, this career path can be quite lucrative. On the other hand, it can be very, very risky.

A Direct Sales Resume Example

In the following resume, you can see how a sales professional positioned herself for a premier sales role with a pharmaceutical company after more than two years of great results and promotion to sales trainer. Eventually she wants to move into sales management, but her immediate goal remains direct sales.

RHONDA McALLISTER

203-481-7943   79 Great Oak Road, Northford, CT 06472   r-mac@yahoo.com

---

PHARMACEUTICAL SALES PROFESSIONAL

#1 in the U.S. — District M.V.P. — Thought Leader Developer — Sales Trainer

Top-producing, award-winning pharmaceutical sales representative with a record of outperforming goals as the #1 producer and sales trainer in the #1 sales area of the country. Recognized for ability to increase market share for all products through innovative and targeted programs that build on solid customer relationships. Delivered consistently successful performance through expertise in sales fundamentals — organization, planning, time management, teamwork, presentation, and relationship building. Aggressive, focused, persistent, and determined in implementing strategies to achieve ambitious goals.

EXPERIENCE AND ACHIEVEMENTS

PHARMA-PRO WORLDWIDE, INC.   **2000–PRESENT**

Northeast Area Sales Trainer, March 2002–Present

Promoted at the earliest possible opportunity within Pharma-Pro (2 years) and tasked with building the sales skills of all 125 sales representatives in 8-state Northeast region.

▶ **Sales Trainer for the #1 Sales Area in the country.**
  - Train, guide, and mentor sales reps through one-on-one field coaching. Noted for delivering consistent, realistic, "no-nonsense" coaching that builds on existing strengths and drives continuous improvement in the full range of sales skills.
  - Deliver week-long business-management and partnership-sales classes attended by all area reps as part of Pharma-Pro's progressive sales-training program.

▶ **Initiator and leader of Area-wide training and education programs that keep Pharma-Pro reps at the forefront of medical issues.**
  - Prepared briefing and recommended responses to Women's Health Initiative research on estrogen and HRT; delivered program to all Fem-Pharma product champions in the Area for roll-out to their teams.
  - Developed and delivered day-long workshop to educate managers on product differences between Pharma-Pro and a key competitor; improved ability of sales reps to answer questions and address competitive issues.

Sales Representative, February 2000–March 2002

Promoted Fem-Pharma, Re-leeve, Re-leeve Weekly, and Xan-pro to primary-care physicians and OB/GYN specialists in Hartford-area territory.

▶ **#1 of 510 sales reps nationally in sales of overall portfolio; #1 in primary product (2000). #14 in overall portfolio; top 3% nationwide (2001).**
  - Achieved 110% of sales quota, 2001.
  - Averaged greater than 10 sales calls daily, 15% above target.
  - Developed and followed tight territory-routing schedule to ensure regular visits to all customers and target accounts. Consistently met or exceeded 80% visit-frequency goal.
  - Chosen by peers as M.V.P., Connecticut district, 2000.

▶ **Thought-leader developer and educational-program coordinator.**
  - Identified, recruited, and developed 2 primary thought leaders in first 2 years as sales rep.
  - Developed a top-5-requested speaker among nearly 200 nationwide.
  - Planned, managed, and effectively promoted peer-to-peer educational events; secured participation from 80% of target accounts.

A direct sales resume.

Sales Representative, continued   **PHARMA-PRO WORLDWIDE**

▶ **Creative problem-solver and leader of innovative targeted sales programs.**
  - Boosted sales of Re-leeve Weekly through inventive product "bundling" that prevented generic switching.
  - Recruited key nurses as product champions/educators within top physicians' offices. Each office increased market share, contributing to sales results of 162% of goal for Xan-pro.
  - Blunted impact of competitive products through educational presentations of hard facts and comparative data. Successfully built market share for Fem-Pharma – in first month after launching educational campaign, grew market share 0.5% while competitor lost 0.4%.
  - Led successful launch of Re-leeve Weekly by developing an action plan for nurse education and patient follow-up.

▶ **Innovative partner/sponsor for teaching hospital residents, building strong professional relationships, and expanding the reach of Pharma-Pro's educational initiatives.**
  - Sponsored and attended OB/GYN Grand Rounds at University of Hartford Hospital.
  - Sponsored residents' Journal Club and delivered educational presentations.
  - Located and sponsored a trained Fem-Pharma speaker as a presenter for an annual post-graduate program. Coordinated Pharma-Pro booth at the 3-day course.

▶ **Connecticut-District Product Champion for Fem-Pharma — #1 drug in the District.**
  - Selected based on product knowledge and sales performance.
  - Initiated an "action challenge" with District team to share successes and strategies; met goal of refocusing and reenergizing team members.

▶ **Mentor to new sales representatives, helping them come rapidly up to speed and continuously improve their field sales performance.**

CONNECTICUT BANK & TRUST, MERIDEN, CT   **1997–2000**
Sales Manager, 1998–2000
Sales Associate, 1997–1998

NORTHEAST FINANCIAL SERVICES, HARTFORD, CT   **1995–1997**
Senior Mortgage Sales Specialist, 1996–1997
Account Executive, 1995–1996

EDUCATION

CORNELL UNIVERSITY, ITHACA, NY
B.S. in Business Administration, 1994

Transitioning from Sales to Marketing

Although it is closely related to sales, marketing is a broader, more big-picture function. Marketing evaluates customer needs, determines which product improvements and new products will be introduced, and selects new markets to enter. Marketing creates the company image and makes sure all advertising and sales support that image. Marketing is more involved in strategy and less in tactical execution of sales programs.

If you enjoy creating plans and strategies, like to influence larger organizations than your own sales territory, and would prefer to get away from the constant challenge to meet new sales goals, you might enjoy marketing. Or you can step into marketing not only to learn this important function, but also to learn the inner workings of your company. This makes a marketing position an excellent career step for salespeople interested in higher-level management positions. A marketing position is a good way to show that you can handle larger and broader responsibilities. You'll have the chance to develop your business-planning skills and work collaboratively with the sales, product development, and financial areas of the company.

The short-term downside to this career path is that marketing positions tend to earn less than sales positions. Ted took a cut in income to take this career step. However, he had his sights set on a longer-term goal and ended up advancing to the executive level.

If you are interested in pursuing a marketing role, the following kinds of activities will help you achieve it:

- Develop innovative sales strategies and share them with sales and marketing managers.

- Suggest new products or new market opportunities.

- Volunteer for a special project that involves working in a team with marketing and other areas of the company.

- Show that you are aware of and interested in more than just your own sales results.

- Ask to be assigned to a new-product launch team.

- Pursue additional education in business and finance (such as an MBA).

Here's an example of a salesperson who transitioned successfully to a combined sales/marketing role and then used that experience to find a pure marketing job. Matt graduated from college with a degree in electronic media and took a job selling advertising for a radio station. In his first year, he concentrated on pure sales and was able to just meet his goals. But then he decided to take a "partner" approach with his accounts, with media advertising being just one part of an overall marketing program. He put together some innovative ideas that used a variety of approaches to build visibility and get results for his clients. As a result, his sales results soared and he found that he really liked the strategy and program-development aspects of the job more than he liked pure sales.

Matt prepared this next resume to highlight his marketing achievements as well as his sales results as he looked for a new job that would be either straight marketing or a combination of marketing and sales. He ended up earning a promotion to develop and manage collaborative marketing programs for his media company.

Matt Robinson

2521 Van Ness Avenue, Vancouver, WA 98685 ● 360-229-4471 ● mr.robinson@hotmail.com

EXPERTISE	**Mass Media Marketing and Sales**
	Strategic marketing and sales professional with a track record of accelerating sales, building strong client relationships, and creating focused marketing programs that meet clients' objectives and deliver results—frequently exceeding projections and generating additional marketing activity.
EXPERIENCE	Columbia Communications, Portland, OR, 1998–2002 **Account Executive,** KSTR-Radio
	Built solid account base from the ground up and increased billings every year by focusing on account management and direct account development.
	Assessed clients' marketing needs and created integrated marketing/advertising programs; assisted key accounts with ad production.
	Developed strong skills in preparing professional proposals and presenting to clients at all levels including senior executives.
Sales Results	• President's Club winner for exceeding annual sales goals. • Increased sales 32% second year, 22% third year, 27% fourth year. • Doubled sales with a key account through strategic marketing planning. • Grew sales from zero to $150K for a local agency; started with one account and brought all accounts into program by year two. • Developed synergistic relationships with sales reps from other media, collaborating to create integrated sales and marketing campaigns that best fit clients' needs.
Marketing	• Developed creative promotion to invigorate attendance figures for a popular weekend attraction… increased attendance 7% in first weekend and motivated business owner to double length of advertising campaign. • Conceived marketing concept and campaign for a new sports event, a race to benefit charity… generated advertising revenue of $40K for one-day event… achieved participation 40% above sponsor's projections. • Created marketing program tie-in with two key accounts designed to build traffic and visibility for both… proposal well received by clients and planned for implementation in spring 2003.
	KCST, Seattle, WA, 1997–1998 **Assistant Program Director** Marketed program offerings to syndicators; assisted Program Director with program selections; analyzed ratings and developed strategies to improve them.
EDUCATION	Bachelor of Arts in Electronic Media, 1998: University of Washington, Seattle, WA
Honors & Activities	• Dean's List • Elected to leadership positions in Phi Delta Omega fraternity: External Affairs (organizing, coordinating, and managing alumni events); Steward (supervising food preparation staff, purchasing food, managing budget and payroll); and Vice President (managing team of 10 officers and serving as liaison to university fraternity council).
VOLUNTEER	Media liaison and in-kind gift solicitor for March of Dimes and American Cancer Society.

A resume for transitioning to a sales/marketing role.

Transitioning from Sales to Sales Management

Moving from sales to sales management is a natural progression for many talented salespeople. And one of the primary qualifications for a job as a sales manager is a track record of success in sales. Other important qualities are the ability to manage, train, and motivate people; good organizational skills and a knack for managing multiple projects at the same time; strong planning skills and the ability to reach goals; and leadership talents. To strengthen your credentials for a move into sales management, look for opportunities to do the following:

- Achieve excellent sales results in your current position.

- Earn sales awards to build your visibility among your company's senior management.

- Train and motivate other salespeople—ask for training opportunities if they don't naturally come your way.

- Lead a new product launch or venture into a new market.

- Show that you have a big-picture viewpoint by identifying opportunities for business growth or recommending new strategies for the sales organization.

- Volunteer for tough assignments and get results.

- Volunteer to make presentations at sales meetings.

- Partner with your accounts and solve their problems by calling in experts from other areas of your company or other suppliers.

- Advance your knowledge of your industry and your company's competitors.

- Increase your knowledge of general business and finance.

One of the myths in this career path is that super salespeople are automatically candidates for sales-management positions. As an aspiring sales manager, you do need to show that you can achieve and over-achieve sales goals. Otherwise, who would want to follow you and let you coach them? However, super salespeople frequently have egos that are too large to allow them to be effective leaders or coaches. That's okay. As long as the super salesperson recognizes this and management recognizes the same, everyone is happy. Ted can relate to this:

> *I was never the salesperson of the year at my company. I was a hard worker and a team player. I always achieved my goals. However, I also demonstrated leadership skills in different ways. For example, I would make product or sales technique presentations at sales meetings. And I could act as the calm voice representing opinions of the sales force. The other salespeople, including the super reps, respected this. When I did get promoted, they were willing to follow my lead.*

The next resume details a rather unusual career progression. Instead of holding a sales job and steadily advancing to sales management, Meredith was thrown into sales management shortly after she joined her company. The region was failing and the sales manager was fired. Meredith had the choice of taking over his job and trying to make it a success or starting all over with a new company. She chose to take over the struggling region and built it into a real success story. Her resume shows both strong sales achievements and sales-management successes, to demonstrate that she is equally capable in both areas.

Meredith Travers

29-A Marlborough Street
Boston, MA 02116

Meredith@email.com
Home: 617-479-8039
Mobile: 617-900-2340

Sales Management Professional

Expert in Key Account Management, Account Retention, Customer Relationship Management, and Leadership of Top-Performing Sales Teams

- Experience encompasses marketing, sales, merchandising, new product launch, brand strategy, and sales team leadership.
- Successful sales background in multiple marketing channels and classes of trade.
- Track record of succeeding in challenging / failed territories through persistence, consistent application of the sales process, and establishment of "above and beyond" customer service as company standard.
- Proven ability to analyze, evaluate, and implement new and innovative strategies to meet changing market demands.
- Expert in all stages of the sales cycle and able to train staff to excel in the sales process.

Professional Experience

GALWAY PRODUCTS, Revere, MA	**Regional Sales Manager**	1995–2002

Hired, trained, and managed 17 sales and administrative staff. Directed all operations for business that grew to $25 million annual revenue.

- **Hired as sales representative and advanced quickly to Regional Sales Manager. Took over failing distributorship and built into consistently profitable performer in highly competitive Northeast region— the category's #1 U.S. market. Grew market share, territory size, and account penetration through effective leadership of sales, marketing, and overall business strategies.**

SALES AND MARKETING

- Created and executed marketing plans that encompassed **multiple channels of distribution and classes of trade.**
- Gained customer loyalty and won preferential treatment for products with key accounts including:
  - **Large national retailers:** Wal-Mart, Target, K-Mart, CVS, Stop & Shop.
    - Secured rare exclusive relationship with Target in Massachusetts.
    - Tripled sales with Wal-Mart by proposing product "striping" rather than horizontal planogram placement. Sales results prompted requests for additional displays in prime store locations.
  - **Resort properties:** Marriott, Hilton, Hyatt, and regional golf resorts.
    - Gained dominant position with a premier Marriott resort through a creative merchandising solution.
  - **Regional wholesalers and distributors.**

SALES MANAGEMENT

- **Built a cohesive team** of sales managers, sales representatives, merchandisers, and office and warehouse staff focused on goal achievement and customer satisfaction.
- Successfully taught **fundamental sales skills and situational problem-solving** to sales team members with widely diverse levels of expertise.
- Conceived and implemented a variety of creative sales incentives to **spur both niche sales and long-term sales growth.**
- Built extraordinary level of teamwork and loyalty among staff; maintained **excellent staff retention.**

Education

UNIVERSITY OF MAINE, Orono, ME	**BS, Business Administration**	1995

A resume for someone who transitioned to sales management almost immediately.

The next resume shows a more traditional career progression, from sales to sales management and finally an executive sales role. Sales results are prominently featured in the achievements listing for every position.

Taylor Jorgenson

2525 Pelican Pathway, Tampa, FL 33614
Home: (813) 554-9943 ● Office: (813) 421-0070
tjorgenson@tampa.rr.com

Sales Management Executive

Delivering impressive revenue gains, profit growth, and market-share increases through strategic sales leadership within high-technology companies.

Consistent record of career achievement in sales and management with high-tech companies and emerging technologies. Strong ability to develop, train, lead, and motivate sales teams to top performance. Record of identifying opportunities and "making things happen" to achieve objectives in highly competitive markets. Experienced in applying CRM and ERP e-business solutions to sales and operations functions across the organization. Innovative and resourceful, with excellent understanding of today's business conditions and ability to develop alliances to promote corporate objectives.

Experience and Accomplishments

BroadNet, Inc. – Tampa, FL   2002–Present

A leading supplier of test equipment and network-management systems designed to ensure the optimal performance and utilization of optical broadband communication networks. $325 million annual revenues.

REGIONAL VICE PRESIDENT (SOUTHEAST REGION)
Create sales strategy and lead combined direct/distributor sales force selling to public network operators, network equipment manufacturers, component vendors, and enterprise network operators. Hold full P&L responsibility for regional performance.

- Led region to top performance in the nation, generating 47% of the total U.S. revenue in the first half of 2002.

- On track to achieve 100% of a $37 million quota in 2002.

- Strengthened performance of sales team through effective leadership, goal-setting, and creation of appropriately motivating incentive and commission structures.

- Focused sales strategy on solution selling to strategic accounts. Developed training programs for account managers targeting strategic accounts across 12 business units.

Electronic Devices, Inc. – Clearwater, FL   1985–2002

Reseller of electronic test and measurement equipment, telecommunications equipment, PCs, and Sun workstations. In sales leadership roles, contributed to growth of company from 40 employees, $7 million revenue to 375 employees, $385 million revenue.

NATIONAL SALES MANAGER (1999–2002)
Drove sales, rentals, and leases of high-tech equipment through national sales force. Directed staff of 80. Formulated strategic marketing plans; established goals; recruited, motivated and managed high-performing sales force.

- Achieved aggressive growth of 20% per year in sales revenue.

- Secured critical distribution channels and initiated partnerships to consistently meet sales goals and market share.

- Designed, developed, and deployed new commission incentive program; increased sales by $2.6 million in first year. Overall, tripled annual sales from $7 million to $21 million.

A more traditional sales-management resume.

NATIONAL SALES MANAGER (continued)

- Instituted "Quality and Excellence" program for clients and staff; key clients included 3Com, Cisco Systems, EMC, Sprint, Dell Computer, IBM, Nortel, and Qualcom.
- Responsible for the asset-management process of a $42 million inventory.
- Championed organizational development and training programs.
- With committee members, analyzed business needs and recommended implementation of SAP ERP software.

REGIONAL SALES MANAGER: FLORIDA (1992–1999)

Coordinated business development throughout industrial, commercial, aerospace, and military markets. Directed fulfillment, administrative, public relations, and marketing activities. Tasked assignments, determined realistic goals, and set priorities to meet deadlines. Provided product training and direction on territory management techniques.

- Managed #1 office in the U.S. in total sales volume for 7 years.
- Achieved over 100% of quota each year while maintaining 35% gross margins on sales; won Regional Manager's Award for greatest business volume ever concluded in a single month.
- Delivered clear, effective, leading-edge presentations.
- Successfully negotiated numerous major corporate contracts.

SENIOR ACCOUNT MANAGER (1985–1992)

Utilized excellent networking and communications abilities to consistently build strong client relationships. Generated customized marketing and presentational strategies to maximize account-development opportunities with largest customers.

- Achieved over 100% of quota each year; won recognition as #1 sales performer in the U.S. until promotion to Regional Sales Manager.
- In competition with 30 other representatives, won 3 national sales contests based on total revenue and new accounts.

BioTools, Inc. – Tampa, FL   1982–1985

World leader in biomedical instrumentation.

SALES REPRESENTATIVE / SERVICE TECHNICIAN

Education

Northeastern University, Boston, MA
BACHELOR OF SCIENCE IN BUSINESS MANAGEMENT

Interests and Activities

Golf / Waterskiing / Tennis

References and additional information available on request.

Transitioning from Sales or Marketing Management to General Management

People who hold senior-management positions such as president, chief executive officer, general manager, and executive vice president might come from very different backgrounds. After all, everyone starts their career on one "ladder" and moves up that ladder or perhaps straddles a couple of different ladders. Sales or sales and marketing is one such ladder, and you'll find that some of the largest and most successful companies in the U.S. have leaders who have come up the ranks in sales.

If your goal is to advance to a high-level general-management role, you'll be wise to do the following:

- Achieve excellent sales results in your current position.

- Be on the lookout for opportunities to broaden your experience.

- Show that you can effectively manage people, projects, and key initiatives.

- Show that you can make presentations to large groups that have impact.

- Volunteer for corporate-level committees, task forces, and special projects.

- Expand your knowledge of the company, industry, and competition.

- Broaden your knowledge of business and finance, perhaps by earning an MBA.

- Seek out mentors in diversified areas of the company.

- Pay careful attention to the bottom line (profits), not just the top line (sales revenue).

- Demonstrate that you can develop overall business strategies and large-scale sales programs.

- Prioritize your activities according to the strategic goals of the company—show long-range vision.

The next resume shows steady career progression, advancing levels of responsibility, and a significant and consistent record of achievement as D.J. Delaney advanced from a territory manager to president of a company in the health-care industry. The resume highlights both sales-management and general-management skills and achievements.

D.J. Delaney

781-942-7525 (H)
781-200-2345 (C)

djdelaney@boston.rr.com

27 Pomeroy Road
Reading, MA 01867

Sales & Management Executive
Healthcare-Industry Products, Services & Technology

Strategic and tactical leader with top-flight career driving profitable growth for emerging and established products and technologies in the healthcare industry. Track record of sustained performance over 15 years in sales and business leadership roles with Spectra Medical Systems, Domino Healthcare, and technology start-ups. Repeated success in building and leading top-performing teams, improving market share, launching new products and services, and leading innovations from concept to market introduction.

General Management: P&L, Strategic Business Planning, Revenue & Profit Growth, Start-Up & Turnaround.
Sales Leadership: Sales Team Recruitment & Leadership, Channel Partnerships & Strategic Alliances, Customer Relationship Management.

- Launched new division that became the only revenue generator for a technology start-up (nearly $2M in less than 1 year).
- In 6 months, reversed faltering zone performance and set the stage for 63% growth the following year.
- In progressively challenging sales/management roles with Spectra Medical Systems, excelled in over-achieving sales goals, building high-performing teams, meeting turnaround challenges, and pioneering sales-training programs. Selected for prestigious management-training opportunity and MBA sponsorship.

Experience

MRI Services, Inc., Reading, MA   2001–Present

President

Co-founded company and acquired the Equipment Services Division of Med-Services.com. Developed strategic business plan and continued the product-development and sales initiatives launched with Med-Services.

- Created new vision for complete Asset Lifecycle Management Solution meeting identified industry need.
- Completed successful Extranet pilot with 12 HCA hospitals and Premier IDN.
- Identified, evaluated, and negotiated strategic partnerships, including a VAR relationship with an industry leader in asset-management software and alliances with "best-in-class" liquidation partners.
- Negotiated profitable sale of MRI to deep-pocket healthcare technology organization.

Med-Services.com, Boston, MA   2000–2001

Vice President / General Manager, Equipment Services Division

Created the vision, strategy, and tactics that led to the successful launch of 2 Web-based software applications that achieved significant momentum and market traction before decision was made to spin off the business. Managed P&L, product development, and hiring/management of cross-functional team of employees.

- Grew division revenue from 0 to $1.8M in 6 months.
- Spearheaded development and launch of the Extranet (a proprietary software program for asset redeployment within healthcare systems) and a liquidation-management program.
- Validated product/technology and secured contracts with 75 hospitals.
- Created go-to-market strategy that emphasized solutions to identified problems in the management and full utilization of costly medical equipment.

Spectra Medical Systems, Chicago, IL   1989–2000

Zone Service Sales Manager, Waltham, MA (7/99–12/99)

Promoted to lead turnaround of $140M zone; challenged to boost revenue, reduce turnover, and develop strategy for sustained growth. Managed a team of 22 in sales of multi-vendor diagnostic imaging/biomedical product maintenance service agreements and productivity solutions. Co-owned zone P&L.

- Developed a strategic business plan that included staff redeployment and performance measurement.
- Created a high-performance sales team, rigorously weeding out underperformers (replaced 50% of field sales staff) and improving training, mentoring, and accountability.
- Laid the foundation for explosive sales growth in 2000: 63% above prior year.

A resume for progressing to general management.

Experience, continued

Spectra Medical Systems continued

Cardiology Region Sales Manager, Chicago, IL (1998–1999)

Chosen for regional leadership role within newly created Cardiology Sales Channel. Recruited, hired, trained, and led a team of 20 diverse, high-potential account managers. Participated in creating and executing the strategic business plan for U.S. Cardiology sales and marketing.

- Led nation in performance at 140% of plan, 1999.
- Created the National Cardiology Program to integrate and train new hires.
- Presented the Cardiology Strategic Business plan at 1999 National Sales Meeting.
- Selected for the Plainfield Medical acquisition/integration team.

Manager, Sales Programs, Chicago, IL (1996–1997)

Recruited into Sales Programs, a management-training opportunity for high-potential employees. Training focused on leadership growth, employee selection and development, and sales training.

- Created and led the Key Talent Pipeline, a turnkey program to proactively recruit, hire, train, and place individuals as "ready now" Account Managers. Promoted 75 U.S. and 18 international candidates out of program in 24 months.
- Led sales-training initiative for U.S. sales division of 500+ representatives.
- Designed and led the delivery of Spectra's Sales Manager Training Program.
- Awarded 1 of 4 company-wide MBA scholarships.

Account Manager, Radiology, Waltham, MA (1989–1995)

Sold diagnostic imaging systems, service contracts, and financing vehicles to CEOs, CFOs, physicians, clinicians, and purchasing managers at hospitals and diagnostic imaging centers in Eastern Massachusetts territory.

- Grew territory from $1M in 1989 to over $12M in 1995; met or exceeded sales quota 5 consecutive years.
- Top 10% of sales performers nationwide, 1993 and 1994.
- Twice finished in "Top 5" of 250 Radiology Account Managers.

Domino Healthcare, Framingham, MA 1987–1989

Territory Manager

- 1988: 118% to plan, #4 in division, >$500K in new gross profit.
- 1987: "Rookie of the Year," #2 in division, 112% to plan.

Education

University of Massachusetts Amherst, MA

MBA, 1998
BS Nursing, 1986

Wrap-up and To Do

A sales position is often the start of a satisfying career. You might choose to remain in direct sales for your entire career, advancing to more prestigious and highly compensated account-management roles, or you might prefer to advance to sales management, marketing, or executive-level positions at your company or other organizations. Your first sales job will give you a great start.

Be aware of the different areas of knowledge and achievement you'll need to demonstrate to move toward your goal. One of the best things you can do is find a mentor at your company, someone who has reached the level you aspire to and can guide your career decisions. Above all, be diligent and dedicated in getting the best possible sales results in each assignment. Success in sales is a requirement for advancement, and being a sales leader is a great way for you to elevate yourself above your peers with similar experience.

APPENDIX

Resources for Your Sales Job Search and Career

In this appendix you'll find some of our favorite resources for information and assistance related to sales careers. Of course, these represent only the tip of the iceberg with regard to what's available through career-assistance professionals, books and periodicals, and Internet resources. But they can get you started and point you in the direction of more, and more specific, resources for your unique needs and interests.

Career Assessments and Personality Type Profiles

For more help on assessing your potential for a career in sales, see the following resources.

Working with Career Coaches

- Be sure to work with an individual who is qualified to assess the results of your personality testing. Our resource for this book's section on the *Myers-Briggs Type Indicator* was Susan Guarneri, a multiply-certified career coach and counselor. You can contact her at Susan@CareerMagicCoach.com (www.careermagiccoach.com).

- Check the membership directory of the Career Masters Institute (www.cminstitute.com) for career coaches and counselors who administer career assessments and can help you interpret the results.

Books

- *Do What You Are,* Third Edition, by Paul Tieger and Barbara Barron-Tieger (Little, Brown, 2001).

- *What's Your Type of Career?: Unlock the Secrets of Your Personality to Find Your Perfect Career Path,* by Donna Dunning (Davies-Black, 2001).

Self-Scored Assessments

Although self-scored assessments do not provide the depth of interpretation you will gain by working with a qualified counselor, you might want to use them as a first step in evaluating your career talents and interests. You can find these self-scored instruments and others at www.jist.com/assessments.shtm.

- *Work Orientation and Values Survey* by Robert P. Brady, Ed.D. (JIST Publishing, 2002).

- *O*NET Career Interests Inventory* (JIST Publishing, 2002).

- *O*NET Career Values Inventory* (JIST Publishing, 2002).

- *Leisure/Work Search Inventory* by John J. Liptak, Ed.D. (JIST Publishing, 1994).

Researching Employers and Industries

The key to finding the right industry and a good employer is to do your research. You can also find out more about salary ranges. The following sources will help you in this research.

Online Research

Dun & Bradstreet
www.dnb.com

Hoovers Online
www.hoovers.com

Monster—Research Companies
http://company.monster.com/

Researching Companies on the Internet
http://home.sprintmail.com/~debflanagan/

Wetfeet Company Profiles
www.wetfeet.com

Reference Books

- *Career Guide to America's Top Industries,* Fifth Edition, by the U.S. Department of Labor, Bureau of Labor Statistics (JIST Publishing, 2002).

- *D&B Healthcare Reference Book* (Dun and Bradstreet Corp., 2002). (See also directories for other industries.)

Compensation

- Research government wage surveys for the industries you're interested in at the U.S. Department of Labor, Bureau of Labor Statistics Web site: www.bls.gov/home.htm.

- Get general salary ranges for free or, for a fee, a precise picture of the salaries for your industry, level, and geographic region. See www.salary.com or www.payscale.com.

Direct-Sales Companies

Do your homework to find the right fit of product, sales method, and company philosophy. Here are a few places to start:

- Amway (www.amway.com)

- Avon (http://avon.avon.com)

- BeautiControl (www.beauticontrol.com)
- Creative Memories (www.creativememories.com)
- Longaberger Baskets (www.longaberger.com)
- Mary Kay (www.marykay.com)
- Pampered Chef (www.pamperedchef.com)
- Weekenders (www.weekenders.com)

Top 10 Sales-Job Web Sites

Provided by Get-a-Job Services (www.getajobservices.com):

1. Advertising Age/Monster.com (jobsearch.adage.monster.com)
2. Jobs4Sales (www.jobs4sales.com)
3. Sales Jobs (www.salesjobs.com)
4. Top Sales Positions (www.topsalespositions.com)
5. Recruit2Hire (www.recruit2hire.com)
6. Sales Classifieds (http://salesclassifieds.com/Main/Default.asp)
7. CareerBuilder (www.careerbuilder.com)
8. SalesTrax (www.salestrax.com)
9. TigerJobs (www.tigerjobs.com)
10. SalesHeads.com (www.salesheads.com)

Resources for Resume Writing and Career Services

- *Sales and Marketing Resumes for $100,000 Careers,* by Louise Kursmark (JIST Publishing, 2000); available at traditional and online booksellers and from JIST's Website at www.jist.com.
- *Cover Letter Magic,* by Wendy S. Enelow and Louise M. Kursmark (JIST Publishing, 2001).

- Career Masters Institute (www.cminstitute.com): Search the directory of members for a professional to help you with career planning, resume writing, and other facets of your career transition.

Resources for Sales Professionals

Even before you land your first sales job, the following resources will be helpful to you.

Professional Associations

- American Marketing Association (www.marketingpower.com)

- Direct Selling Association (www.dsa.org)

- Sales and Marketing Executives International (www.smei.org)

- Toastmasters (www.toastmasters.org)

- Hospitality Sales and Marketing Association International (www.hsmai.com)

Magazines

- *Sales and Marketing Management* (www.salesandmarketing.com)

- *Sales and Marketing Strategies & News* (www.salesandmarketingmag.com)

- *Sales Pro Magazine* (www.salespromagazine.com)

- *Selling Power* (www.sellingpower.com)

- Pharmaceutical Representative (http://pharmrep.com)

Training

These are just a few of the many Web sites that offer free resources including newsletters, sales tips, tele-seminars, online training opportunities, and information about in-person sales training.

- Dale Carnegie Training (www.dale-carnegie.com)

- Industrial Ego Sales Training (www.industrialego.com)

- Just Sell (www.justsell.com)

- Sales Training Institute (www.salesinstitute.com)

- Sales Training International (www.saleshelp.com)

- Sales Training University (www.sales-training-management-institute.com)

- Wilson Learning (http://wilsonlearning.com)

Sales Strategy

There are literally thousands of books on "how to sell" or "how to sell better." These are just a few of our favorites.

- *Swim with the Sharks,* by Harvey Mackay (Fawcett, 1996).

- *The Sales Bible,* by Jeffrey H. Gitomer (William Morrow & Co., 1994).

- *SPIN Selling,* by Neil Rackham (McGraw-Hill, 1998).

- *Advanced Selling Strategies,* by Brian Tracy (Fireside, 1996).

- *Cold Calling for Women: Opening Doors and Closing Sales,* by Wendy Weiss (DFD, 2001).

- *How to Master the Art of Listing and Selling Real Estate,* by Tom Hopkins (Prentice Hall Press, 1991).

- *How to Master the Art of Selling,* by Tom Hopkins (Warner Books, 1994).

- *Ziglar on Selling: The Ultimate Handbook for the Complete Sales Professional of the Nineties,* Zig Ziglar (Ballantine Books, 1993).